EMBRACED
BY THE
SPIRIT

The Untold Blessings
of Intimacy with God

CHARLES R.
SWINDOLL

ZONDERVAN® A WORTHY BOOK

ZONDERVAN.com/
AUTHORTRACKER
follow your favorite authors

231.3
SWI

ZONDERVAN

Embraced by the Spirit
Copyright © 2010 by Charles R. Swindoll

This title is also available as a Zondervan ebook.
Visit www.zondervan.com/ebooks.

This title is also available in a Zondervan audio edition.
Visit www.zondervan.fm.

Requests for information should be addressed to:

Zondervan, *Grand Rapids, Michigan 49530*

Library of Congress Cataloging-in-Publication Data

Swindoll, Charles R.
   Embraced by the Spirit : the untold blessings of intimacy with God / Charles R. Swindoll.
       p.   cm.
   ISBN 978-0-310-32754-7 (hardcover, jacketed)
   1. Holy Spirit. 2. Spiritual life—Christianity. I. Title. II. Title: Untold blessings of intimacy with God.
   BT121.3.S95   2010
   231'.3—dc22   2010029817

Contents

∾ Introduction ∾

If you are truly and completely fulfilled in your spiritual life, seldom frustrated, and rarely dissatisfied, this book is not for you. No need to read further.

But if, like me, you long for a more intimate and uninterrupted relationship with the living God, where you and He are "in sync" and where you regularly sense His presence and experience His power, let's walk through these pages together.

Most of the people you sit with in church live with a persistent, nagging fear that they are missing out on something in their walk as a believer. Their intellectual faith is intact—but their intimacy with God is missing. No one could argue with them about what they believe, but it's been a long time since their heart has stirred with fresh faith. To make matters even worse, they haven't explored any new places in God's Word for years. And lest exposed as "weird," they keep their distance from anything related to the Holy Spirit. Don't go too far down that road or you'll be labeled "emotional" or "falling into error."

I call that tragic. If you are one of the vast number of Christians who have never known the joy, the sheer ecstasy, of walking more intimately with God, yet have known there was more, so much more . . . my hope is that these pages will draw you in, calm your fears, encourage you to be held tighter by His embrace. I understand what you have been going through and I welcome you as a fellow pilgrim who is weary of a sterile, unproductive, predictable existence. Jesus' promise of an "abundant life" surely includes more than that!

Most of us are intrigued by the Holy Spirit. Like a moth to a lamp, His bright warmth attracts us. Our desire is to draw nearer, to know Him intimately. We long to enter into new and stimulating dimensions of His working—but yet we hold back. We're hesitant . . . fearful of being wrong or misunderstood. I know that was once true of me, and I suspect you often feel the same.

I have discovered that often one of the best ways to arrive at the right answers is to start with the right questions. Perhaps that is what first attracted me to a disarming little book titled *Dear God: Children's Letters to God.*

A little girl named Lucy asked God: "Dear God, are You really invisible or is that just a trick?"

Norma asked: "Dear God, did You mean for a giraffe to look like that or was that an accident?"

One of my favorites was asked by Nan: "Dear God, who draws the lines around all the countries?"

Anita asked, "Is it true my father won't get in heaven if he uses his bowling words in the house?"

Hilarious, charming, innocent... and oh, so perceptive! Don't you wrestle at times with similar questions?

I saved Seymour's question for last: "Dear God, How come You did all those miracles in the old days and You don't do any now?"[1]

Is that true? Certainly it may appear to be the case. "Dear God, have all those great and mighty things ended? Is that all there is to the Spirit's ministry? Have we reached the end of His meaningful presence and powerful workings?"

These are valid questions. Here are some more that beg to be answered. We'll explore each one in greater detail in our journey together:

- Who is the Holy Spirit?
- Why do I need the Spirit?
- What does it mean to be filled with the Spirit?

- How do I know I'm led by the Spirit?
- How does the Spirit free me from sin?
- Can I be prompted by the Spirit today?
- Does the Spirit heal today?
- How can I know—really experience—the Spirit's power?

We will explore the answers to each one of these questions in the chapters that follow as we discover for ourselves real-to-life reasons we need the Spirit. We will also learn the incredible difference He can make in the way we conduct our lives on a personal basis.

During my growing-up years, including my years in seminary, I kept a safe distance from most things related to the Holy Spirit. I was taught to be careful, to study Him from a doctrinal distance but not to enter too closely into any of the realms of His supernatural workings. Explaining the Spirit was acceptable and encouraged; experiencing Him was neither. Embracing Him was out of the question. Today, I regret that. I have lived long enough and ministered broadly enough to realize that drawing near to Him is not only possible, it is precisely what God wants.

My great hope in these pages is to step away from the heat of theological battle that analyzes and criticizes and move quietly and closely to the One who has been sent alongside to help. He longs to empower you and me with His dynamic presence. He is ready and able to change our attitudes, warm our hearts, show us how and where to walk, comfort us in our struggles, strengthen us in the weak and fragile places of our lives, and literally revolutionize our pilgrimage from this planet to paradise. Inner transformation is His specialty.

Candidly, this is a book for the heart much more than for the head.

I invite you to enter the journey on a personal level. Other studies can be found that approach this topic on a more cognitive level, looking at theological nuances and exhaustively researching every detail. But in our journey through these pages together, rather than restricting God's Spirit to a library shelf, let's invite Him into the room. The Spirit of God was sent, ultimately, to be engaged in our everyday lives . . . to be experienced *intimately*. God intended our relationship to be close—growing in depth and nearness.

Never forget this: the Holy Spirit is interested in transforming us from the inside out. His nearness sets that in motion. He is at work in dozens of different ways, some of them supernatural. He is interested in showing us the Father's will. He stands ready to provide us with the dynamics necessary for experiencing satisfaction, joy, peace, and contentment in spite of our circumstances. Embracing the Spirit gives us the correct perspective for entering into those (and so many other) experiences. Isn't it time for that to become a reality?

I invite you to come along and journey with me. We've got nothing to fear, only great joys to be discovered when we follow His lead.

Charles R. Swindoll
Frisco, Texas
Summer 2010

WHO IS THE HOLY SPIRIT?

One of my most unforgettable moments happened when I was about ten years old. My father served our country during World War II in a plant in our hometown, building all sorts of interesting equipment for the massive tanks, fighter planes, and bombers that defended us in lands far away. Dad worked too long and too hard. As a result he suffered a physical breakdown, and on its heels came an emotional trauma that puzzled everyone, including the doctors.

I was convinced in my heart that my dad was going to die. He may have had such thoughts too, because one night he called me into his room for a somber father-son talk, spoken in terminal terms. I remember leaning hard against his bed, listening carefully to a voice that was hardly more than a whisper. I thought I was hearing him for the last time. He gave me counsel on life—how I should live, how I should conduct myself as his son. The counsel wasn't long, and then I left and went across the hall to the room that I shared with my older brother. All alone, I lay across my bed and sobbed, convinced that I would never see my dad alive again.

That scene haunts me. Even though my dad recovered to live three decades more, I still remember the night he talked with me.

Something very significant is wrapped up in our final words. Consider that night in Jerusalem when the Lord and His disciples gathered for the Passover Seder—what we call "The Last Supper." Less than twelve hours after the disciples sat beside the Savior during that meal, Jesus was nailed to a cross; a few hours later, He was dead. Jesus understood the significance of those moments and the importance of His last counsel. And so He gave His disciples exactly what they would need to carry them through the rest of their days. In that little room they pushed aside wooden cups and bowls, and every eye fell on Him and every ear leaned in to hear His voice. Their grief hardly allowed them to take in the last words of their Lord as He taught them how they might live on . . . without Him.

Recorded by the disciple John—one who had sat by the Lord's side at that meal and who had meditated upon those events for sixty years before expressing them in his Gospel—the comfort and instruction that fell from our Lord's dying lips comes alive in John 13 through 17.

Two Secrets about the Christian Life

Jesus told His men two secrets—two pillars of truth that support all other truths about the Christian life . . . truth that would bring life into focus after His death. The first related to Him and had to do with something that happened when He came. The second relates to us and has something to do with what would happen when He left . . . and what has since happened.

First, the truth about Him: Jesus told the disciples that the secret of His victorious life was His vital union with His Father. He spoke of His Father repeatedly as He talked that night. He told them that when He came to earth it was with the Father's blessing, it was in the Father's power, and it was through the Father's guidance that He was able to minister. In addition, it was the Father's will that He proclaimed the Father's Word. Because there had never been a break in that vital union, He had been able to live a perfect life, qualifying Him to die as the sin offering for man.

But He didn't stop there. The second secret was about His followers: that our victorious life is connected to our vital union with the Holy Spirit. If we would be habitually empowered by the Spirit that indwells us, we could know the kind of life He had lived. Ian Thomas described this well: "The life that He lived qualified

Him for the death that He died. And the death that He died qualifies us for the life that He lived."

Jesus told us that the life He lived is possible to be lived day after day when we draw upon the strength of the Spirit of God who lives within us. Read this as *new* news for yourself: through His Spirit, we can actually live like Christ.

No doubt the disciples were confused to hear about "a Spirit." Their minds were probably still whirling with His declaration, *"I'm going away."* They sat paralyzed, riveted to that statement, unable to form any of the questions they would later ponder. They were in shock. Jesus pointed out that they weren't even curious about where He was going. They couldn't cope with the news of His departure, just as I couldn't, as a little boy, cope with the possibility that my dad would be gone by morning. Wrestling with that tragedy and unable to get beyond it, I dissolved into tears.

So did the disciples. "Sorrow filled [their] hearts" (John 16:6). The Greek word for *sorrow* here means "grief"— devastating pain that accompanies the loss of someone we love. Jesus understood all that they were experiencing. He saw that grief and fear had gripped them.

We all want very much to give the impression that we can handle anything that comes. We want to appear secure, even when we feel very insecure. The big lie is that "We can handle everything." The truth is, deep down within each of us, we long to be kept. We ache to be held securely. When some earthquake takes that security from us, the moorings of our foundation shift. It happens when we face the possibility of a terminal illness or the imminent death of a loved one or danger on the battlefield. How many soldiers go berserk on the landing craft before they ever hit the water? The imminence of danger or separation brings about feelings of desperate insecurity. That's what happened with the disciples. And Jesus said, "Look, men, sorrow has filled your heart. Grief has paralyzed you. I understand."

But He didn't abandon them in that desperate place. He promised, "I will not leave you as orphans; I will come to you" (John 14:18).

We are able to read that calmly . . . but try to imagine the disciples hearing it for the first time. Their stomachs must have churned at the word *orphan*, for that is exactly how they felt. For more than three years they had been inseparable. Jesus was there when they awoke. He stood with them through virtually every situation they faced. When they called for help, He was nearby, ready to step in. When they said "Good night," He quickly responded. Suddenly all that would change. He was leaving them— permanently. And though they were adults, the sting of His departure left them feeling orphaned.

I told you about that night when I thought my dad was leaving our family. To our surprise, he recovered and lived another thirty-five years, even surviving my mom and living to see us all grow up. Nevertheless, his departure from this life in 1980 marked a passage in my life after which things would never be quite the same. No more visits. No more phone calls. No more opportunities to sit and talk through something and to have him listen and respond. In a strange way since that day, there are occasions I feel orphaned. I still miss being able to see my father, to hear his voice, to watch him respond.

That was how the disciples felt. No more meals together. No more discussions beside the sea. No more quiet talks around the fire at night. No more shared laughter . . . or tears . . . or watching Him handle some thorny situation. *Orphaned.*

I love Jesus' compassion for them in that moment. He carefully chose His words. "I won't leave you orphaned . . . I have a solution." Plan B was already in motion. The answer Jesus gave them was the person of the Holy Spirit.

"I WILL NOT LEAVE YOU ORPHANED"

I will ask the Father, and He will give you another Helper [literally, another of the same kind], that

He may be with you forever; that is the Spirit of
truth, whom the world cannot receive, because it
does not see Him or know Him, but you know
Him because He abides with you and will be in
you. (John 14:16–17)

Aha! Jesus promised them that His replacement
would be "another Helper." Namely, the Holy Spirit.
And when that other Helper came, He would become
an integral part of their lives. He would reside within
them. Unlike Jesus, who had only been *with* them, He
(the Spirit) would be *in* them. Huge difference! Not too
many days hence, when the Spirit arrived, He would
slip inside them and live within them forever. No more
temporary companionship; the Spirit's presence would be
(and still is) a permanent presence. It had never been like
that before. Not even in the lives of those Old Testament
greats. But from now on . . . yes!

Jesus had to leave in order for the Spirit to begin His
permanent indwelling. Jesus made that clear: "But I tell
you the truth, it is to your advantage that I go away; for
if I do not go away, the Helper will not come to you; but
if I go, I will send Him to you" (John 16:7).

The question that comes to mind is, *Why was it
advantageous for Jesus to leave? Why is it more beneficial for
us to have the Holy Spirit than Christ Himself?*

That's not too difficult to answer. Jesus Christ, while on earth, inhabited a body. Therefore He could be only one place at one time. When He was in Nazareth, He was not in Jerusalem. When He was near the northern shores of Galilee, He could not be walking along the Dead Sea. He could only be one place at one time. However, when He left the earth and sent the Spirit, the Spirit of God, being omnipresent (the everywhere-ness of God), could fill and empower with the same power a man in Palestine, a woman in Syria, and yet another individual in faraway Italy. At the same moment you experience power like Jesus experienced from the Father, a believer in Angola or in Alaska or the southern tip of Australia can experience that same power at the very same time.

"It's advantageous that I go," said Jesus. "That way you don't have to be with Me physically to have My strength. I'll give you that inner strength you need, and it will never leave." What a great plan! The reaction was fear; the solution was the Spirit of God.

Embracing the Person of the Holy Spirit

Notice Jesus referred to the Helper as "He" or "Him," not "It." To most folks, the person, work, and ministry of the Holy Spirit are little more than a mystery. He is not only invisible but also a bit eerie . . . especially when, for years,

He has been referred to as "It" and formally addressed as the Holy *Ghost*. The whole concept is difficult to get our arms around.

All of us have had earthly fathers, so trying to understand the concept of a heavenly Father is not that difficult. In traditional homes, the father is the one in charge, making the big decisions and ultimately responsible for the family's overall protection, direction, leadership, and stability. There are exceptions but in the final analysis, it is Dad who casts the final vote. We respect and honor God the Father. We worship Him in the majesty and beauty of His holiness.

We identify much more easily with Jesus. Although He is the Son of God, He was born as a human being and grew up alongside His parents, much like we did. Because He was a flesh-and-blood person, we have a tangible mental image of Christ. Even His role as the Son of God is fairly clear to us. Our familiarity with His suffering and death causes us to feel close to Him and grateful for Him. He is the One who points to the Father. He is the One who implemented the Father's plan. We not only love Jesus, we adore Him.

But the Holy *Ghost*? To many, He is still the divine "It." Not even changing His title to "Spirit" helps that much. Certainly to the uninitiated the name sounds weird. If His name is vague, it is no surprise that most find

His work and ministry mysterious. And since those who attempt to explain His workings are usually theologians who are often notoriously deep and unclear themselves, no wonder most people don't have a clue in understanding what He is about. Small wonder we don't feel intimately related to Him.

But no more! God is not passive. He didn't just hope we would be okay; He is proactive, sending His Spirit so our security is certain.

MOVING FROM THEORETICAL TO RELATIONAL

Candidly, I am just as guilty as those complex-thinking theologians who have attempted to "explain" the inscrutable Spirit of God. Way back in the 1960s I taught a course on the third member of the Trinity. When I picked up my pen to write this book, I thought it might be helpful to glance over those old notes. My immediate problem was locating them. Had I filed them under *H* for "Holy Spirit"? No. How about *S* for "Spirit"? Nope. Maybe they were tucked away in my subject file under the letter *G* as in "Holy Ghost." Wrong again. Or *T* for "Trinity." Not a chance.

I stayed at it until I unearthed them . . . filed under *P* for *Pneumatology.* Amazing! That tells you a lot about how I approached the Holy Spirit five decades ago: strictly theoretical and theological . . . not at all relational.

Don't get me wrong. There is nothing—absolutely nothing—wrong with theology. Sound doctrine gives us strong roots. Those who lack such stability can easily fall into extremism and error. However, it won't cut it to track a subject this intimate from an impersonal distance, keeping everything safely theoretical and coolly analytical. There has been too much of that already. What we need is a much more personal investigation of the intimate workings of the Spirit—we need to be embraced by the Spirit without losing our anchor on theological truth.

Admittedly, some of the Spirit's workings seem more theoretical than experiential. But a closer look makes them very personal. For example:

- *The Spirit is God—co-equal, co-existent, and co-eternal with the Father and the Son.*

- *As a child of God, you have God Himself living inside you.* St. Augustine, who found himself yielding to sin on one occasion, turned and ran. Finally, all alone, he stopped and put his head in his hands and said, "Oh, soul, dost thou not know that thou art carrying God around with thee?"

- *The Spirit possesses all the attributes of deity.* All that you have heard about God—His everywhere-ness,

His all-powerful-ness, His all-knowing-ness—can be said of His Spirit. So when you need strength, the Spirit is right there to give it. When you need confidence . . . faith . . . comfort . . . you can get all you need from His Spirit.

- *The Spirit regenerates the believing sinner.* Your salvation, made possible because of Jesus' death on the cross, is personally accomplished in your heart through God's Spirit. He makes alive that immaterial part of you that was stone-cold dead in sin. He brings you to life in a new and eternal way.

- *The Spirit baptizes us into the universal body of Christ.* You have a new identity, a new family. You've got relatives you don't even know about. You are connected by a common bond that takes you all the way back to the cross. Because of the Spirit, you and I are members of God's family.

- *The Spirit indwells all who have been converted.* You are never alone. Your day-to-day life takes on an eternal dimension because He lives in you. Life's catastrophes can be weathered because you have a different purpose for living.

- *The Spirit seals us, keeping every believer securely in the family of God.* You should have no fear of losing what God accomplished on your behalf . . . beginning with your salvation. You didn't do anything to earn it; the Spirit guarantees you won't lose it. He's got you covered.

And that's just a start!

These truths are so deeply personal that it's going to take us a while to unpack them, but it's a wonderful journey. What we're about to discover is the practical difference the Spirit can make in our lives on a personal and lasting level.

I've been a pastor for nearly fifty years. Year after year, talking with folks before I preach or while standing in front of the church after a worship service, I'm able to get a handle on the questions that people are asking. Without exaggeration, the majority of the issues on people's hearts can be answered with a practical understanding of how God's Spirit works within the life of the Christian.

My emphasis will be on the practical side of the Holy Spirit—seldom-mentioned dimensions of His work within us individually and His ministry among us collectively. Why? Because these are the things that give us an edge on living in a sin-cursed world, surrounded by people who have lost their drive for life. It is when these things come alive in us that we become unique instruments in God's hands. I believe that's what you really desire. Candidly, I do too! We have everything to gain and nothing to lose by allowing the truth to emerge. It's the truth, remember, that sets us free.

The inescapable fact is this: most (yes, *most*) Christians you and I know have very little dynamic or joy in their lives. Look at them. Ask them! They long for depth, for passion, for a satisfying peace and stability instead of a superficial relationship with God made up of religious-sounding words without feelings and on-going struggles without healings. Surely there is more to the life of faith than church meetings, Bible study, religious jargon, and meaningless prayers. Surely the awesome Spirit of God wishes to do more within us than what is presently going on. There are scars He wants to remove. There are fractured feelings He wants to heal. There are insights He longs to reveal. There are profound dimensions of life He would dearly love to open up. But none of the above will happen automatically—not as long as He remains a sterile, untouchable blip on our theological screen.

We need to allow ourselves to be embraced by Him. We need the security that comes from being completely surrounded by His protection and power. He is the comforting Helper, remember? He is the Truth Teacher, the Will-of-the-Father Revealer, the Gift Giver, the Hurt Healer. He is the inextinguishable flame of God, my friend. *He is God.* To remain at a distance from Someone that vital is worse than wrong; it is downright tragic.

REMOVING THE RESISTANCE BETWEEN US AND HIM

Doesn't all of this sound appealing? Haven't you longed for such fortitude, such confident faith? These traits were never meant to be restricted to century-one saints. Nowhere in the Scriptures do I find a statement that limits the Spirit's presence or dynamic to some bygone era. The same One who promised a handful of frightened followers new dimensions of divine enablement is anxious to fulfill that in us today.

Frankly, I'm ready for that kind of enablement, aren't you? You and I need it, and it is ours to claim . . . so let's claim it!

I must make a brief but honest confession: a practical, personal look at the Spirit does not come naturally to me. I was raised by a very stable, consistent mother and predictable father who provided a solid home where my brother, sister, and I grew up securely. We were taught to love God, believe in Christ, trust and obey the Bible, and be faithful in church attendance. Much of my theology was hammered out on the anvil of those early years at home.

As I grew up, my roots were strengthened in the fundamentals of the Christian faith. My training in seminary drove those roots even deeper. By the time I graduated from Dallas Theological Seminary, I had many convictions and few questions, especially in the realm of the Holy Spirit. I thought I had the subject "knit up," as they say.

But during a lifetime of ministry that has taken me around the United States and to many countries abroad, I have found that the work of the Holy Spirit continually keeps me off balance. I'm not alone in that. Those in church leadership seem afraid the Spirit is going to do something that we can't explain. I've found that disturbs many folks . . . but I'll admit it energizes me. I've come to realize that there are dimensions of the Spirit's ministry I have never tapped and places in this study about which I know very little. I'm on a strong learning curve. I have witnessed a dynamic power in His presence that I long to know more of firsthand. I now have questions and a strong interest in many of the things of the Spirit I once felt were settled. To say it plainly, I am *hungry* for Him. I long to know God more deeply and more intimately. I'm not alone.

The *Amplified Bible* describes the same desire in the great apostle Paul:

> [For my determined purpose is] that I may know Him [that I may progressively become more deeply and intimately acquainted with Him, perceiving and recognizing and understanding the wonders of His Person more strongly and more clearly], and that I

may in that same way come to know the power out-flowing from His resurrection. (Phil. 3:10)

This intimate knowledge and practical power is the work of the Spirit, alive in me. I long to have my life enriched inside the circle of His embrace. I genuinely long to experience for myself the untold blessings of intimacy with God Himself made possible by His Spirit.

I've come to realize that only a fine line separates the mystical from the profound. I'm not bothered by the mystery. I know that we as men and women are limited by all that we can understand. Let's not try to unscrew the inscrutable! There's no reason to add to the mystery with our own conjecture. But I'm convinced that the more we allow "the Spirit of truth" to guide us into all the truth (John 16:13), the more He invites us to travel much deeper into these intimate and mysterious realms. The more we can keep the real world in view, the more we will feel embraced by the comforting and reassuring presence of the Spirit. There's nothing to be afraid of.

DISCOVERING THE SPIRIT'S SIGNIFICANCE

That said, may I ask you, have you ever been shown from the Scriptures just how significant a role the Lord intended the Holy Spirit to play in your life? Before bringing this chapter to a close, let me help you see three contributions He makes, without which life is reduced to dull and gray.

His Unparalleled Dynamic among Us

Think back to that scene in Jerusalem just hours before the cross. Jesus promised that the Spirit would come. But when? The disciples probably pushed that question to the back of their minds as that terrible weekend unfolded. What's interesting is this: when they saw the risen Lord a few days later, He brought it up again.

> Gathering them together, He commanded them not to leave Jerusalem, but to wait for what the Father had promised, "Which," He said, "you heard of from Me; for John baptized with water, but you will be baptized with the Holy Spirit not many days from now." So when they had come together, they were asking Him, saying, "Lord, is it at this time You are restoring the kingdom to Israel?" He said to them, "It is not for you to know times or epochs which the Father has fixed by His own authority; but you will receive power when the Holy Spirit has come upon you; and you shall be My witnesses both in Jerusalem, and in all Judea and Samaria, and even to the remotest part of the earth." (Acts 1:4–8)

In those last moments before the Lord ascended, His mind was on the Spirit. Naturally, He wanted to say good-bye to His closest friends. He wanted to reassure them: "You will receive power when the Holy Spirit has come upon you" (v. 8). Not *if* the Spirit came, but *when*. And immediately upon His arrival, power would transform their lives. He promised that!

Now, Jesus did not say that power would begin to exist at that point, for power had always been one of God's characteristics. Power initiated creation. Power opened the Red Sea. Power brought water from the rock and fire from heaven. In fact, that same magnificent power had brought Christ back from beyond at His resurrection. But those supernatural manifestations were not what He was promising. The disciples would not be creating worlds or parting seas or taking the place of God.

Christ promised them *enabling power* that would transform them from the inside out. Another kind of power, as A. T. Robertson correctly observed: "Not the 'power' about which they were concerned (political organization and equipment for the empire on the order of Rome) . . . this new 'power' *(dunamin),* to enable them (from *dunamai* to be able), to grapple with the spread of the gospel in the world."[1] Jesus was saying, in effect, "You will receive a new enablement, a new dynamic, altogether different from what you have ever experienced before."

This transforming power also included an inner confidence, sometimes to the point of invincibility, regardless of the odds they would face. F. F. Bruce, in his splendid volume on the book of Acts, stated that "they would be clothed with heavenly power—that power by which, in the event, their mighty works were accomplished and their preaching made effective. As Jesus Himself had been anointed at His baptism with the Holy Spirit and power, so His followers were now to be similarly anointed and enabled to carry on His work."[2]

The power (I prefer to use the term *dynamic*) that Jesus promised the disciples directly—and us indirectly—was the Spirit's unparalleled help and enablement, which would immeasurably surpass their own human ability. Think of it! That very same dynamic is resident within every Christian today. But where has it gone? Why is it so seldom evident among us? What can be done to get it in motion as it once was? It's those questions that prompted me to write this book.

His Affirming Will for Us

In His statement prior to His departure, Jesus included an additional promise to His disciples. "You shall be My witnesses," He said (v. 8). The Spirit would free their lips so that they would witness consistently of Him. First in Jerusalem, where they would be located when the Spirit came. Next in Judea and Samaria, the surrounding regions beyond the capital city. Ultimately "even to the remotest part of the earth" (v. 8). The Spirit's presence would spur them on, enabling them to speak openly and boldly of their Savior.

He still longs to do that within and through us today, affirming God's will for you and for me.

A quick glance at the fourth chapter of Acts reveals the results of this Spirit-filled dynamic: perseverance. Peter and John had been preaching in the streets of Jerusalem, where they were later arrested, confronted, and threatened by the officials. Undaunted by the threats, those two disciples stood toe-to-toe with the officials. Their calm perseverance and remarkable courage did not go unnoticed: "Now as they observed the confidence of Peter and John and understood that they were uneducated and untrained men, they were amazed, and began to recognize them as having been with Jesus" (Acts 4:13).

Why? Why would the religious officials marvel at untrained and unlearned men? What impressed them? It was the disciples' firm resolve. Their thoughts might have been: *These are a different category of humanity. They are not like the soldiers we deal with or the politicians or our fellow officials.* Frankly, they recognized that these were Jesus' people—men who had once been with Jesus. How would they know that? The dynamic.

Not long afterward, the Jewish supreme court called the disciples back and told them in no uncertain terms to knock it off.

> "We gave you strict orders not to continue teaching in this name, and yet, you have filled Jerusalem with your teaching and intend to bring this man's blood upon us." But Peter and the apostles answered, "We must obey God rather than men." (Acts 5:28–29)

Clearly, that is persistent, invincible dynamic. Normally the official setting of a courtroom intimidates people. But not these men.

Remember Acts 1:8? "You will receive power." You'll be witnesses. You'll have perseverance to stand firm, regardless. That promised power is now on display.

A few moments later these same Spirit-enabled men set the record straight:

> The God of our fathers raised up Jesus, whom you had put to death by hanging Him on a cross. He is the one whom God exalted to His right hand as a Prince and a Savior, to grant repentance to Israel, and forgiveness of sins. And we are witnesses of these things; and so is the Holy Spirit, whom God has given to those who obey Him. (Acts 5:30–32)

And what happened? Did they lick their wounds and curl up in some cave until the situation cooled down? Were they frightened and disillusioned? Weeks earlier they would have been. Not now. Even after threats and brutal beatings, "they went on their way from the presence of the Council, rejoicing that they had been considered worthy to suffer shame for His name. And every day, in the temple and from house to house, they kept right on teaching and preaching Jesus as the Christ" (Acts 5:41–42).

The Spirit's enablement—that's heaven-sent, transforming power! Get this: the same Spirit who filled believers in the first century is ready to fill us today. That same dynamic can be ours, the same boldness and determination, invincibility and perseverance in the midst of danger.

His Permanent Presence within Us

Put yourself back again with the disciples in that Upper Room in those last intimate moments with Jesus. Let's relive the scene. Feel the heaviness in the air. Hang on His final words. Identify with the growing panic in the disciples' hearts. *You're going away?* They sat stunned. Felt orphaned. Some may have wept. *You're leaving us alone?*

Picture their Savior, their Friend, Jesus. Imagine how His heart rushed to their comfort. *No, I'm not leaving you alone.* "I will ask the Father. He will give you another

Helper, that He may be with you forever—the Spirit of truth, whom the world can't receive. He abides with you and will be in you" (John 14:16–17).

Pause right now. Realize this: when your heart is troubled, the most devastating, demoralizing, paralyzing thought you can ponder is, "I'm all alone." Isn't that true? "Nobody cares" comes next.

But, child of God, I've got wonderful news: you are *never* alone. God cares immeasurably about you. He gave you His Spirit to be with you. When you came to know Christ, He took up His residence and began living inside you. The very word *helper* (*parakletos*) means "one called alongside to help."

He enables you to face today's trials.

He empowers you to meet tomorrow's demands.

He gets you past the divorce.

He guides you to your mate.

He goes with you to the funeral home.

Thursday, Friday, Sunday, Monday, He is with you. Wherever you are—hospital room, dorm room, at home alone, in a difficult work environment, with a sick child, standing by a fresh grave—you have an inner Helper. He has "come alongside" to assist you. The Spirit of God has been provided to comfort as nobody else can. He loves you. He'll never leave you. He supports and strengthens you. And because of His indwelling presence, you have an amazing life open before you.

I love how my friend Eugene Peterson described the work of the Spirit in Ephesians 3. Read this slowly, preferably aloud. His words describe what we will learn together in the coming pages:

> I ask [the Father] to strengthen you by his Spirit— not a brute strength *but a glorious inner strength*— that Christ will live in you as you open the door and invite him in. And I ask him that with both feet planted firmly on love, you'll be able to take in with all Christians the extravagant dimensions of Christ's love. Reach out and experience the breadth! Test its length! Plumb the depths! Rise to the heights! Live full lives, full in the fullness of God." (Eph. 3:15–19 MSG, emphasis mine)

That is what happens when you and I are embraced by His Spirit. That's why He came. Let's start there as we begin to experience the untold benefits of intimacy with our great God!

WHY DO I NEED THE SPIRIT?

In 1983 John Sculley quit his post at PepsiCo to become the president of Apple, a role in which he served for ten years. He took a big risk leaving his prestigious position with a well-established firm to join ranks with an unproven little outfit that offered no guarantees, only the excitement of one man's transforming vision. Sculley says he made the risky move after Apple cofounder Steve Jobs goaded him with the question, "Do you want to spend the rest of your life selling sugared water or do you want a chance to change the world?"

The original disciples were a handful of unlikely misfits, nothing more than a "rather ragged aggregation of souls," as Robert Coleman put it in his *Master Plan of Evangelism*.[1] But the remarkable fact is that they were the same ones who later "turned the world upside down" (Acts 17:6 KJV) according to the testimony of people in the first century.

How can anyone explain the transformation? Was it some crash course they took, some upbeat seminar on leadership? No. Then maybe it was really the work of angels, but the disciples were given credit for it. No, the biblical record clearly states that it was the same group of once-timid men Jesus had trained. Perhaps some high-powered "heavenly drug," some miracle-inducing chemical, was inserted into their bodies that changed the men overnight . . . *Enough!*

There is only one intelligent answer: it was the arrival and the empowerment of the Holy Spirit. He alone transformed those frightened, reluctant men into strong-hearted, unintimidated, invincible messengers of God. Instead of feeling abandoned and orphaned, instead of spending the rest of their lives with "sugared water," they became directly engaged in changing the world. Once the Spirit took up residence with them, once He was given complete control of their lives, He put His agenda into full operation, and they were never the same. They embodied His dynamic. They no longer held back. Not one of them stood in the shadows or looked for excuses not to obey their Lord's mandate to "go . . . and make disciples of all the nations" (Matt. 28:19). Once "another Helper" (John 14:16) came, transformation occurred—immediate transformation.

A Brief Glance at the "Orphaned" Disciples

To appreciate this transformation as fully as we should, we need before-and-after portraits of the men who walked with Christ. Let's start with the scene we visited in chapter 1—the Last Supper.

Judas had left. The meal had been eaten. The taste of bread and wine was still in the disciples' mouths as their Lord began to unveil the reality of His departure. Their stomachs churned with the thought of going on without Him. They were troubled, even though He urged them, "Do not let your heart be troubled" (John 14:1). They were confused, as Thomas's question reveals: "Lord, we do not know where You are going, how do we know the way?" (John 14:5). Another in the group was bothered about the change in plans as he asked, "Lord, what then has happened that You are going to disclose Yourself to us and not to the world?" (John 14:22).

Later, Peter denied Him . . . and he was the leader of the group (Mark 14:66-72)! Ultimately, when push came to shove, "all the disciples left [Jesus] and fled" (Matt. 26:56). Every last one of them deserted their Master.

At His resurrection they were surprised at the thought of His body not being in the tomb. That same evening, after knowing of His resurrection, the disciples hid in fear behind closed doors. Why? They were hiding "for fear of the Jews" (John 20:19). If that wasn't enough, even after He came among some of them, Thomas firmly resisted, declaring he had to witness everything firsthand or (in his own words) "I will not believe" (John 20:25).

Troubled, confused, bothered, disloyal, fearful, doubting . . . These men were anything but valiant warriors for Christ. Prior to the Spirit's transforming work, to put it bluntly, they were wimps! To them, when the original game plan was aborted, the mission was considered unaccomplished.

I often return to Coleman's realistic description of the disciples. It is anything but flattering.

> What is more revealing about these men is that at first they do not impress us as being key men. None of them occupied prominent places in the Synagogue, nor did any of them belong to the Levitical priesthood. For the most part they were common laboring men, probably having no professional training beyond the rudiments of knowledge necessary for their vocation. Perhaps a few of them came from families of some considerable means, such as the sons of Zebedee, but none of them could have been considered wealthy. They had no academic degrees in the arts and philosophies of their day. Like their Master, their formal education likely consisted only of the Synagogue schools. Most of them were raised in the poor section of the country around Galilee.

Apparently the only one of the twelve who came from the more refined region of Judea was Judas Iscariot. By any standard of sophisticated culture then and now they would surely be considered as a rather ragged aggregation of souls. One might wonder how Jesus could ever use them. They were impulsive, temperamental, easily offended, and had all the prejudices of their environment. In short, these men selected by the Lord to be His assistants represented an average cross section of the lot of society in their day. Not the kind of group one would expect to win the world for Christ.[2]

You may not appreciate such a forthright portrayal of the disciples, but from what I read of them in the Gospel accounts, it is accurate. Prior to the coming of the Spirit and His transforming presence in their lives, they bore all the marks of men least likely to survive, to say nothing of succeed.

An Enlightening Discovery of Personal Transformation

Jesus knew His men much better than they knew themselves. He knew Judas was deceptive and Peter was rash. He knew Thomas struggled with doubt and that John was a dreamer. He knew how petty and competitive they were . . . how selfish and fragile. He knew the final eleven thought of themselves as fiercely loyal, but when the chips were down, they would slink into the shadows. He knew that a new dynamic was imperative if His mission for the establishment of the church and the evangelization of the world had any hope of being accomplished. Therefore, when He promised "another Helper," He meant One who would transform them from the inside out. He knew that the only way they would ultimately do "greater works" than He had accomplished would be through the Spirit's presence and power.

Little did the disciples realize how much they lacked. Most of them (perhaps all of them) thought they had more going for them than was the case. Peter, remember, assured his Lord, "I will lay down my life for You," and "Even though all may fall away, yet I will not" (John 13:37; Mark 14:29). What a comedown when they later realized that they were not nearly as resilient or loyal or courageous as they had assured Him they would be.

We've all been there, haven't we? About the time we get out on a limb thinking we're pretty capable, we get sawed off by a sudden and embarrassing discovery. At that point we realize we aren't nearly as effective or competent as we had convinced ourselves we were.

Max DePree gives a splendid example of this in his classic work *Leadership Jazz*. The story goes that a German machine tool company once developed a very fine bit for drilling holes in steel. The tiny bit could bore a hole about the size of a human hair. This seemed like a tremendously valuable innovation. The Germans sent samples off to Russia, the United States, and Japan, suggesting that this bit was the ultimate in machining technology.

From the Russians, they heard nothing. From the Americans came a quick response inquiring as to the price of the bits, available discounts, and the possibility of a licensing arrangement.

After some delay, there was the predictable, polite response from the Japanese complimenting the Germans on their achievement, with a postscript noting that the Germans' bit was enclosed with a slight alteration. Excitedly the German engineers opened the package, carefully examined their bit, and to their amazement discovered that the Japanese had bored a neat hole through it.[3]

When the Spirit of God bored His way into the lives of those awaiting His arrival in that upstairs room somewhere in Jerusalem, His transforming presence was immediately evident. When we look at the events that transpired in the early part of the book of Acts, we can see at least four changes among those who received the Spirit.

1. *Their human frailties were transformed into super-natural gifts and abilities.*

From the moment the Holy Spirit arrived, nothing about the disciples remained the same. When His power, His dynamic (the Greek term used here is *dunamis)*, fell upon them, they even spoke in another language.

> When the day of Pentecost had come, they were all together in one place. And suddenly there came from heaven a noise like a violent rushing wind, and it filled the whole house where they were sitting. And there appeared to them tongues as of fire distributing themselves, and they rested on each one of them. And they were all filled with the Holy Spirit and began to speak with other tongues, as the Spirit was giving them utterance. (Acts 2:1–4)

Try to imagine those phenomena occurring back-to-back.

- A noise, an incredibly loud roar (the Greek term is the word from which we get our English word *echo),* not unlike the sound of a violent hurricane unleashing its howling, earsplitting fury on some coastal village.

- A large "ball" of fire spontaneously separating into

smaller flames, each in the shape of a tongue that came to rest upon each person in the room.

• Each of the individuals simultaneously "filled with the Holy Spirit," their lips flowing words they had never spoken before in languages they had never learned.

This experience completely revolutionized their lives. Those who had been troubled and fearful no longer struggled with those feelings. The once frightened, unsure, confused, timid men never again evidenced such inadequacies. From that time on they were bold in faith and confident in their God. They were transformed.

Suddenly they were able to speak in languages not their own. So clear and accurate were those languages that those who heard them were shocked.

And when this sound occurred, the crowd came together, and were bewildered because each one of them was hearing them speak in his own language. They were amazed and astonished, saying, "Why, are not all these who are speaking Galileans? And how is it that we each hear them in our own language to which we were born? . . . We hear them in our own tongues speaking of the mighty deeds of God." (Acts 2:6-11)

It is noteworthy that the original term used for *language* in verses 6 and 8 is the Greek word *dialektos,* from which we get *dialect.* Remarkable! Those untrained, monolingual Galileans were suddenly able to communicate in the native dialects of individuals from regions far removed from Galilee.

And if that were not enough, some in the group were given the supernatural ability to touch another life and restore physical health. On one occasion, Peter and John were going to the temple to pray. They passed a man who had been lame from birth, begging at the temple gate. Peter told the man,

> "I do not possess silver and gold, but what I do have I give to you: In the name of Jesus Christ the Nazarene—walk!" And seizing him by the right hand, he raised him up; and immediately his feet and his ankles were strengthened. With a leap, he stood upright and began to walk; and he entered the temple with them, walking and leaping and praising God. (Acts 3:6–8)

Before we get the idea that these men suddenly "glowed" with some kind of aura or in some other way appeared different, however, let's hear the testimony of Peter:

While he was clinging to Peter and John, all the people ran together to them at the so-called portico of Solomon, full of amazement. But when Peter saw this, he replied to the people, "Men of Israel, why are you amazed at this, or why do you gaze at us, as if by our own power or piety we had made him walk?" (Acts 3:11–12)

Clearly, Peter and John were still just plain Peter and John. They didn't promote themselves as miracle workers or divine healers. They seemed to be as amazed over this as those who witnessed what had happened. Having been transformed by the Helper whom Jesus had sent, the disciples did not turn the scene into a man-glorifying sideshow.

2. *Their fearful reluctance was transformed into bold confidence.*

Remember an earlier scene when these same men, afraid of being found out by the Jews, hid silently behind closed doors? The last thing they wanted was to be pointed out as followers of Jesus. They were frozen in fear.

No longer. According to Acts 2:40, they poured into the public streets of Jerusalem preaching Christ and urging total strangers to repent and to believe in the name of Jesus. Later, when Peter and John had been arrested and were being questioned, their quiet confidence did not go unnoticed. Their interrogators knew they were uneducated and untrained men, but "they were amazed, and began to recognize them as having been with Jesus" (Acts 4:13).

The followers of Jesus didn't look any different physically. They didn't suddenly become learned men. Nor were they abruptly made to be more cultured and sophisticated. No, they remained rawboned fishermen and what we might call a couple of "good ole boys." But deep within their beings, down inside, they were nothing like they had been. They were transformed.

3. *Their fears and intimidation were transformed into a sense of invincibility.*
Webster states that *intimidation* means timidity, being afraid, overawed, deterred with threats. These men, having been invaded by God's Spirit, were none of the above.

- Instead of running from the public, they ran toward them.

- Instead of hoping not to be seen, they exhorted total strangers to repent.

- Instead of being frightened by insults, warnings,

and threats, they stood face-to-face with their accusers and did not blink.

- Even when called before the Council, the supreme ruling body of the Jews, this handful of "uneducated and untrained men" stood like steers in a blizzard. They weren't about to back down, even if they were forced to stand before some of the same prejudiced and cruel judges who had unjustly manipulated the trials against Jesus of Nazareth. They refused to be overawed. Such invincible courage!

Where does one get such boldness today? From studying at Oxford or Yale or Harvard? Hardly. How about from reading the biographies of great men and women? That may stimulate our minds, but it cannot transform our lives. Then perhaps the secret of such boldness is a mentor, someone whose walk with God is admirable and consistent. Again, as helpful as heroes and models may be, their influence cannot suddenly infuse us with invincible courage. The Spirit of God alone is able to make that happen.

It was not until He came and filled those frail and frightened men with His supernatural dynamic that they were genuinely and permanently changed deep within—transformed.

4. *Their lonely, grim feelings of abandonment were transformed into joyful perseverance.*

On the heels of their second arrest, Peter and John let out all the stops. When they were told to stop talking about Jesus, they looked their opposition squarely in the eye and responded, "We must obey God rather than men" (Acts 5:29). Not what the accusers wanted to hear. So they flogged the apostles and again ordered them to speak no more in the name of Jesus, then released them. The Jewish leaders must have thought, *That ought to do it.*

But it didn't. As we saw earlier,

> So [Peter and John] went on their way from the presence of the Council, rejoicing that they had been considered worthy to suffer shame for His name. And every day, in the temple and from house to house, they kept right on teaching and preaching Jesus as the Christ. (Acts 5:41–42)

The *Amplified Bible* says they were "dignified by the indignity" (v. 41).

The flogging, the warning, and the threat merely fueled their determination. In fact, they left rejoicing. And upon their return to their company of friends, joy filled everyone's hearts—not sadness, not disillusionment, but joy. The wimps had become warriors!

The Spirit of God may have reminded them of the words of the now-departed Lord: "In the world you have tribulation, but take courage; I have overcome the world" (John 16:33). In fact, Peter himself would later write:

> Beloved, do not be surprised at the fiery ordeal among you, which comes upon you for your testing, as though some strange thing were happening to you; but to the degree that you share the sufferings of Christ, keep on rejoicing, so that also at the revelation of His glory you may rejoice with exultation. (1 Pet. 4:12–13)

Quite likely he was recalling that day when he and John had been dragged before the Council and unfairly beaten. Instead of wondering, "Why did the Lord leave us alone?" or "Where is He when we need Him?" their joyful perseverance won the day. No resentment. No feelings of abandonment. No pity party for PLOM (Poor Little Ole Me) members.

Why? Because the disciples had been radically changed, not merely motivated or momentarily mesmerized. They were transformed.

A Straightforward Analysis of How It Happened

But how? What did it? How could these same men who had earlier run for cover now stand tall, refusing to be backed down or even beaten down?

One possible explanation that comes to mind is *positive thinking*. Maybe one or two in the little band of disciples looked around and said, "Now that Christ has left, it is time for us to look at the bright side of things and be responsible."

Very, very doubtful. Positive thinking doesn't go very far when folks are getting the skin beaten off their backs—and it certainly doesn't keep them rejoicing in the midst of such torture. Nor does positive thinking suddenly change a person who is naturally and normally intimidated into one who is invincible. Having a positive attitude is a wonderful thing, but it is unable to bring about wholesale transformation.

Another possibility is a *better environment*. Maybe things lightened up. Perhaps the public had a change of heart and became more open and willing to accept responsibility for crucifying Christ. Caesar himself may have decided that followers of Christ were not really that much of a concern to the mighty Roman Empire.

You're smiling. You know that things got increasingly more hostile, more intense.

Well, perhaps someone *taught a seminar* on "How

to Endure Suffering: Twelve Steps Toward a Successful Life."

No, you know better.

If you ever go to Rome, spend some time in the catacombs. Walk slowly through the narrow, labyrinthine paths that lead deep into the bowels of that subterranean world and you will see sights you'll never forget. You will feel like groaning as you stare at slender little berths where broken bodies were placed. You may even see the writings or touch the sign of the fish or a cross, a crown, or some other equally eloquent, albeit mute, reminder of pain. As you brush along those ancient graves in silence, much of the superficial stuff you read today about being happy through suffering will seem terribly shallow. At the same time, the few signs that pulsate with true triumph in Christ will take on new meaning. What you will witness firsthand will be the evidence of transformed lives.

The Best (and Only) Conclusion

No course was taught. No cheerleader led the disciples in mind-bending chants that gave them a positive attitude. No change in environment brought about their transformation. Clearly, it was the Spirit of God . . . nothing else. It was the life-changing, attitude-altering, dynamic power of the living Lord that swept over them, permanently residing within them.

Remember Jesus' promises? Let me quickly review several of them:

> I will ask the Father, and He will give you another Helper, that He may be with you forever; that is the Spirit of truth, whom the world cannot receive, because it does not see Him or know Him, but you know Him because He abides with you and will be in you. I will not leave you as orphans; I will come to you. (John 14:16–18)

> But you will receive power when the Holy Spirit has come upon you; and you shall be My witnesses both in Jerusalem, and in all Judea and Samaria, and even to the remotest part of the earth. (Acts 1:8)

God kept His word. And the disciples were never the same.

A PROBING QUESTION ONLY YOU CAN ANSWER

So much for first-century disciples of Jesus. Fast-forward to today. Is the Spirit of God being allowed to transform *your* life? In case you think that's an irrelevant question, read the opening words of Romans 12:

> Therefore I urge you, brethren, by the mercies of God, to present your bodies a living and holy sacrifice, acceptable to God, which is your spiritual service of worship. And do not be conformed to this world, but be transformed by the renewing of your mind, so that you may prove what the will of God is, that which is good and acceptable and perfect. (vv. 1–2)

Don't miss the twofold command: "Do not be *conformed* . . . but be *transformed*" (emphasis mine).

Are you honest enough with yourself to answer my question? Are you allowing the Holy Spirit to transform your life?

There are only two possible answers: yes or no. If your answer is no, there are two possible reasons. Either you do not have the Spirit within you (i.e., you're not a Christian), or He is there but you prefer to live life on your own. I'll address that in more detail in the pages that follow. For now . . . let me urge you to do some soul searching.

My concern is the Spirit's main agenda: Are you allowing Him to transform your life? If not, why not?

Could it be that you're afraid of what that might look like?

Just imagine what it means to have the presence of the living God within you. The third member of the Godhead, the invisible, albeit powerful, representation of deity, is living inside your being. You think you can't handle what life throws at you? You think you can't stand firm or when necessary stand alone in your life? You think you can't handle sin's temptations? Truth be told, you're right—you can't . . . alone. Neither could those disciples. But with the very power of God put into operation, you can handle it. As a matter of fact, the weight will all be shifted from you to Him. It's wonderful.

Jesus promised the men in the Upper Room that "when He, the Spirit of truth, comes, He will guide you into all the truth" (John 16:13). Not only does that mean that the Spirit will make Scriptures clear to you, but He will also take circumstances and give you insight into them. In other words, He transforms your mind. He takes life's pressures and uses them to mature you. He transforms your character. He nurtures you. He comforts you when you're fractured with fear. He transforms your hope. He tells you there's another day coming when you can't see the end of the tunnel. He gives you a reason to go on when it looks like death is near. He transforms your thinking. He transforms your heart. He transforms your perspective.

Does that sound fearful or crazy to you? No, not to me either. The Spirit's transformation has become my highest pursuit and I pray it is also yours. Your transformation— the Spirit's main agenda. Allow yourself to be embraced by the Spirit today.

∽ 3 ∽

WHAT DOES IT MEAN
TO BE FILLED WITH THE SPIRIT?

I don't know of anyone who's more magnetic or more attractive than an authentic Christian. The longer I live, the higher priority I place on authenticity. As an authentic believer, you live what you believe. You speak the truth. You love generously. You admit failure quickly. You acknowledge weakness without hesitation. Among our highest callings as Christian men and women is that we know who we are, we accept who we are, and we are who we are.

Are you? The absence of such authenticity explains why the world around us has stopped believing a lot of our claims. They've seen too much phoniness, which gives them good reason to question the authenticity of today's Christianity.

My hope for this chapter is for us to understand how to live that kind of authentic life, resulting in our lives verifying the truth of Holy Scripture.

First and foremost, we must realize that the authentic Christian life is impossible and unexplainable without the Holy Spirit. God's Spirit is the power behind authenticity . . . behind genuine living of every description. It has nothing to do with your circumstances. That's what makes it so phenomenal.

If you don't know Christ as Savior, as hard as you may try, you simply do not—you cannot—know what I'm talking about. Matter of fact, chances are good you will call all of this foolishness. That's understandable; as 1 Corinthians 2:14 explains, since you don't have the Spirit within you, you can't accept the things of the Spirit of God. They are "moronic," a good translation of the Greek word for "foolish."

But the sad truth is most Christians know little of this kind of abundant, Christlike, authentic life, either. Very few believers are accurately taught from Scripture how to let the Spirit fill them. There might be a lot of talk on the street and in the pews, and a lot of equally phony displays of the Spirit's power, but precious few truly understand the process.

So here's the secret—which is really no secret at all. Tucked away in the fifth chapter of Ephesians is the clear and unmistakable direction about what it means to be filled with the Spirit.

WHERE'S THE POWER?

Earlier, in chapter 1, we eavesdropped on a conversation Jesus had with the disciples after the Last Supper. It was their last meal together before Jesus went to the cross. The Lord promised to send His Spirit so that He could always be with them (and us). John 14:16 says, "I will ask the Father, and He will give you another Helper, that He may be with you forever." In fact, He said a little later, He would not only be with the disciples, "He . . . will be in you" (v. 17).

So Jesus promised the Spirit at that last meal, and reminded them as He left the earth that His followers would "receive power when the Holy Spirit has come upon you; and you shall be My witnesses both in Jerusalem, and in all Judea and Samaria, and even to the remotest part of the earth" (Acts 1:8).

We live our lives with an eye toward the world around us. We're not supposed to be a closed clan, a tight little clique of people living unto ourselves. Cults do that, but not the church. As an authentic, Christlike community, we live for the purpose of reaching the entire world with the message of the Savior.

People are watching . . . but they're not always impressed. They want to see that what we believe makes a transforming difference in our lives. More than just coping with life's challenges, they want to see a remarkable response that cannot be forged. The difference in your life comes down to how, as a Christian, you respond when . . .

- you face a dreadful trial from which you cannot escape

- a doctor tells you she's concerned about the X-rays

- the phone rings in the night with news about someone you love

- you are the target of a complicated and ugly attack

In that topsy-turvy moment the Christian's best response is, "God, I need You." You need Him to step in, calm your fears, and take charge. More than all that, you need the confidence that He is there at that very moment. You're not expecting an audible voice from heaven or a vision of the future in hi-def. Not that. What you need most is the unmistakable inner reassurance that He is there, that He cares, that He is in full control.

For this we *need* the Spirit. And for this we *have* the Spirit.

The Spirit in you, and in control, makes a noticeable difference. Too often we concede with just getting by . . . when the Spirit wants to enable us with an abundance of what we may need. How many times have we settled for a little relief when the Spirit promises to give us a peace that is so pervasive it passes understanding (Phil. 4:7)?

When you have experienced His supernatural power, you remember it for a lifetime.

WHEN THE SPIRIT TOOK OVER

Allow me to tell you a personal story that speaks to this. It's really every parent's fear. Some years ago my phone rang on a warm, quiet Friday afternoon. It was someone at the high school telling me that our oldest daughter, Charissa, had been in an accident. She had been practicing a formation with her cheerleading squad when the whole human pyramid collapsed. Charissa had been at the top and, consequently, fell the farthest, hitting the back of her head with a sharp jolt. Her legs and arms had gone numb. She was unable to move even her fingers. After notifying the paramedics immediately, the school official had called me.

I raced to the school, not knowing how seriously our daughter had been injured. En route, I prayed aloud. I called out to the Lord like a child trapped in an empty well. I told Him I would need Him for several things: to touch my daughter, to give her mother and me strength, to provide skill and wisdom to the paramedics. Tears and feelings of fear were near the surface, so I asked the

Lord to calm me, to restrain the growing sense of panic within me.

As I drove and prayed, I sensed the most incredible realization of God's presence. It was almost eerie. The pulse that had been thumping in my throat returned to normal. By the time I reached the school parking lot, not even the swirling red-and-blue lights atop the emergency vehicle disturbed my sense of calm.

I ran to where the crowd had gathered. By that time the paramedics had Charissa wrapped tightly on a stretcher, her neck in a brace. I knelt beside her, kissed her on the forehead, and heard her say, "I can't feel anything below my shoulders. Something snapped in my back, just below my neck." She was blinking through tears.

Normally, I would have been borderline out of control. I wasn't. Normally, I would have been shouting for the crowd to back away or for the ambulance driver to get her to the hospital immediately! I didn't. With remarkable ease, I stroked the hair away from her eyes and whispered, "I'm here with you, sweetheart. So is our Lord. No matter what happens, we'll make it through this together. Your mother is on her way. We're going to be with you, no matter what happens. I love you, honey." Tears ran down the sides of her face as she closed her eyes.

I followed the ambulance in my car, again sensing the Spirit's profound and sovereign presence. Cynthia joined me at the hospital, where we waited for the X-rays and the radiologist's report. We prayed, after I told her of my encounter with the Spirit's wonderful presence.

In a few hours we learned that a vertebra in Charissa's back had been fractured. The doctors did not know how much nerve damage had been done. Neither did they know how long it would take for the numbness to subside—or if, in fact, it ever would. The physicians were painfully careful yet honest with their words. We had nothing solid to rely on, nothing medical to count on, and nothing emotional to lean on . . . except the Spirit of God, whose presence was tangible with us through the entire ordeal.

Sunday was just around the corner (it always is). By Saturday night I was exhausted, but again God's Spirit remained my stability. In human weakness and with enormous dependence on the Lord, I somehow put a sermon together, which I preached on Sunday morning. The Lord gave me the words, and He proved His strength in my weakness. I was told later by our media folks that more people requested a copy of that sermon than any other up to that date. I found that amazing. It was a demonstration of the Spirit's power through a very weak vessel.

Here's what happened, plain and simple. God the Holy Spirit filled me, took full control, gave great grace, calmed fears, and ultimately brought wonderful healing to Charissa's back. Now, a couple decades later, the only time her upper back hurts is when she sneezes. If I am with her when that happens, I usually look at her and ask, "Did that hurt?" Invariably, she nods and says, "Yeah, it did." I smile, she smiles back, and for a moment we mentally return together to that original scene where she and I felt a very real awareness of the Spirit's presence.

All of us desperately need the Spirit's filling in those crisis moments. At such times, our natural strength will crumble.

But you also need to be filled with His Spirit in your normal, everyday-life moments. I'm not sure where authenticity speaks the loudest—perhaps it's a tie. Most of life happens in the middle and that's also where we need the Spirit's filling. The Spirit of God provides us with the power to live a normal Christian life—an everyday, believable, Christlike life, authentic from one day to the next.

THE CHRISTIAN LIFE IS LIKE MARRIAGE

I like to compare the authentic Christian life to a marriage. A normal, solid, reliable marriage is not filled every day with soft, romantic music wafting through the rooms of your home, accented by dreamy, scented candles and bouquets of fragrant roses. A good marriage doesn't mean you frequently sit for hours in a bubbly hot tub, kissing and hugging each other. After awhile, both of you can't even fit in the same tub together . . . and you don't even want to. After so many years together, truth be told, that's just not normal.

What is normal? A Christian life that's real is transformational—like we saw in the last chapter. The Spirit of God does more than just "help you out a bit." He provides the complete enablement to live a life that those without Christ can't even imagine. It includes such practical things as the power to control your tongue, the strength to face each day's challenges, the ability to clean up your thoughts, a way to guard yourself from temptation so that you don't plunge after one lustful lure then another. The authentic Christian life offers you hope beyond the downward drag of the flesh. Let's face it: the Spirit life and the flesh life are always in opposition to one another.

The Christian Life Is Like a Car

Two things are essential for you to enjoy any car that you buy. First is a set of keys. The key lets you into the car. It'll help you open the trunk or the glove box or, whenever necessary, to lift the hood on the car. It's what you need to crank up the engine. You can admire the car from the outside, or even sit quietly inside it, but you're not going anywhere without the keys.

What the keys are to the car, conversion is to the Christian life. You don't enter the Christian life because you're born into a Christian family or because you attend a church where the Bible is taught, or even because you learn verses from a book called the Bible. You enter the Christian life through only one way: the key—Jesus Christ. John wrote it this way, "He who has the Son has the life; he who does not have the Son of God does not have the life" (1 John 5:12).

You either have the key that gets you into the car or you don't. You either have life in Christ or you don't. There is no in-between ground to stand on.

The second essential you need for your car is fuel. Don't try to save money by filling up your tank with water from your garden hose and hope your car will run. The engine was designed to run on fuel. What the fuel is to the car, the Spirit of God is to the authentic, normal Christian life.

Colossians 2:6 explains it like this: "As you have received Christ Jesus the Lord, so walk in Him." As you have received Christ (that's the key that gets you inside), so walk in Him (that's the fuel, the Spirit of God engaging your life in an authentic manner).

Jesus said that He would send the Spirit of God, and by sending Him, He would provide the power to live as His witnesses. Some folks today have taken that word *power* and made it walk on all fours. Today, there's power everything. There's "power evangelism," whatever that is. There is "power prayer," "power preaching," "power healing," "power encounters," "power ministry" for every size and shape there may be. You can even wear "power ties" to carry out your "power ministry" on "power Sundays." If ever a word has been overused and abused, it's *power*.

We get our words *power* and *dynamic/dynamite* from the Greek *dunamis*. It's a word that refer to "divine enablement." Because I have the Spirit, I have within me sufficient enablement to handle my flesh. I can't handle it on my own. All the time I was without Christ I couldn't, but once I came to Christ, I received the key to the car. I also received the fuel for the tank, which enabled me to engage the gears. When the Spirit of God takes over, His power overcomes the fleshly forces within me—the drive to react, the drive to strike back, the drive to get even, the drive to throw a temper fit, the drive to have my own way, and on and on the list goes. This is the work of the Spirit as He now provides divine enablement.

Your Body: The Holy Spirit's Temple

First Corinthians 6:19 paints an interesting metaphor that further explains the indwelling of the Spirit: "Your body is a temple of the Holy Spirit." What does that mean? Simply, He lives inside your life. You don't have to ask for Him to come in. He came in when you trusted Christ . . . when you were converted. And because He dwells within, His desire is to be in control of your lips and eyes and ears and actions and thoughts and reactions and motives.

Never forget this: Jesus promised that the Spirit will be in you (John 14). If you're a Christian, you don't need to pray "Lord, send me Your Spirit" or "Please be with us today." Those are very common prayers . . . but they are unnecessary. He *is* with you. In fact, His Spirit lives within every believer.

Since the believer's body is considered the "temple of the Holy Spirit," it stands to reason that He should be glorified in it and through it. After all, He owns it. We do not belong to ourselves, we are the Lord's. As our Master, He has every right to use us in whatever way He chooses. In living out the Christian life, we have one all-important objective: to glorify God in our body.

When you operate your life from this perspective, it changes everything. That explains why it is so important to view every day—sunup to sundown—from the spiritual dimension. When we do, we begin to realize that nothing is accidental, coincidental, meaningless, or insignificant. Things that happen to us are under our Lord's supervision because we are His, and we are to glorify Him, regardless. Since we belong to Him and His Spirit lives in us, we are in good hands. Truth be told, we occupy the best possible situation on earth.

This means that words like *accident* or *coincidence* should be removed from our vocabulary. Seriously! When events transpire that we cannot understand or explain, we are reminded that we are not our own. Rather than being anxious, frustrated, or confused, we should step aside and allow His Spirit to fill us with the divine fuel we need to press on . . . to honor Him in those events . . . ultimately, to glorify Him.

Are you ready for more? When you are inhabited by someone else, you're able to accomplish what you could never do on your own.

I love the piano but when I sit down to play, those black-and-white keys groan. The piano knows it's not being played well. However, if I were to bring into our home the maestro Van Cliburn and have him sit down at that same piano and begin to play, our piano would sound the way a piano ought to sound. I would stand back, shake my head, and say, "How wonderful! Our piano is so happy and so are all of us who are listening to you today."

Let's go further. What if Van Cliburn said to me, "You know what, Chuck? I have the supernatural ability to give you my skill and my heart so that you can play like I play."

I would say, "You're kidding."

"No. Are you ready?"

And I'd say, "Yeah, of course!"

He'd do his magic and suddenly, I'd be Van Cliburn! I would sit down and begin playing Chopin's "Polonaise," Beethoven, Bach, and all kinds of fancy Mozart finger work. I'd be improvising up and down the keyboard on some of the great hymns as well. It would be wonderful. I'd be *amazed* at this ability to do what I could never have done on my own.

Then I'd start thinking, *Hey, I'm pretty good. Hey, honey, Cynthia . . . come in here and listen to me!* And suddenly, my Chopin pieces would change back into "Chopsticks."

Why? Because when you're operating in the power of the Spirit, you don't operate for your own glory. If anything is being carried out, it's being carried out for God's glory. But when the flesh takes over, the enablement of the Spirit ceases.

First Corinthians 6:19 reminds us that "you are not your own." If you try to play Chopin on your own, you're going back to playing "Chopsticks." In a simple and fragmented way, that is what it is to be filled by the Spirit. You're not operating on your own. You must operate your life under the control of the One who has come to live within you. Your goal in life is not to get what you want—but to do what He wants you to do. It's not all about you—it's about Jesus. Beware all those self-help books that tell you that you can rise to some great heights on your own; if you're not careful, your pride will kick in and take charge. When you look deep enough, what you'll find is nothing but gross depravity.

You're not your own; you've been bought with a price. Isn't that a helpful reminder? In other words, God is still God and I am still not.

So, what are we supposed to do? We're to "glorify God in [our] bodies" (1 Cor. 6:20). Think like this: "Lord God, I'm Yours. You have gifted me in ways that I wouldn't have ever expected, and I thank You. I'm here to serve You. May my service be for You and for Your glory. May it be authentic. May it magnify Your name. I want to honor You, O God."

In order for me to live the life God would have me live, I need His fuel. I need His empowerment. I need His transforming power. I rely on His control. Without His life, I'm sunk.

Be Careful How You Walk

If I could, I would offer this counsel to every Christian: "Be careful how you walk" (Eph. 5:15). Our ultimate goal is to glorify God. That takes care. Be careful to pay attention. Be careful to listen to His Word. Be careful to pray. Be careful to seek His help.

Furthermore, be careful how you walk because you're being observed. It would amaze us to know how many people are watching. After all these years you'd think I'd have learned this by now. Like when I slip anonymously into a grocery store on one of those late-night trips and I'm not dressed like I ought to be, and I think, *Well, nobody will be there who knows me.* So I step in quietly and a little girl waves and chirps, "Hi, Pastor Swindoll."

Or even worse, people are watching when I'm behaving badly . . .

Several years ago Cynthia and I hosted a cruise with our *Insight for Living* listeners. On the plane going to our departure city, she had ticked me off about something not that important but I sat there with a fair amount of (fleshly) control. A little later the argument continued as we walked down to get on the cruise ship. So I said to her, "Step over here a second." Off to the side, I decided to set her straight in no uncertain terms. I "unloaded the truck" as I got everything out of my system. I thought, "There! That oughta do it!"

Then I turned around and faced about seventy-five people waiting in line—the people coming with us on the cruise, watching us with their eyes and mouths wide open. It wasn't a good moment!

"Be careful how you walk." Be careful what you say. You know what should bother me more than seventy-five people who were shocked at my conduct? My out-of-control behavior grieved the Holy Spirit. That was no way to talk to my wife. I wasn't careful how I walked or with what I was saying. What's needed is wisdom to conduct my life, as Ephesians 5:15 goes on to say, "not as unwise . . . but as wise."

Furthermore, when you are under His control, you are "making the most of your time, because the days are evil" (v. 16). God knows that's true. And when you're under God's control you are able to discern His will for you (v. 17).

How can we walk as we ought to walk? How can we be wise when we tend toward being less than wise? How can we make the most of our time? How can we understand the will of the Lord? We need His empowerment, His enablement, His power. That's what the next verse in Ephesians is all about.

WHAT IT MEANS TO "BE FILLED"

I don't know of a more important verse in the New Testament for the Christian than Ephesians 5:18— honest, no exaggeration. This verse tells the believer how to live an authentic, empowered life: "And do not get drunk with wine, for that is dissipation, but be filled with the Spirit."

It begins with a negative command: "Don't get drunk with wine, for that is dissipation" (which means excess, existing hopelessly out of control). When you're drunk with alcohol, you lose control. You also lose self-respect and the respect of others. "Don't get drunk."

A positive command follows: "But be filled with the Spirit." Let's be very careful to analyze precisely what this says. To do so, I want to underscore four significant factors about the construction of that command. Careful, meticulous Bible study is important if we hope to grasp what God's Word says.

1. *Be filled with the Spirit.*

This is a command, not a suggestion. It's an urgent imperative, not a casual option. This instruction is part of a longer list of instructions; we have no more freedom to ignore this "be filled with the Spirit" than we do to overlook the ethical commands that surround it, such as "work hard," "speak the truth," "be kind," and "forgive."

"Be filled" is a command, which means I play a part in it. For example, I cannot be filled with the Spirit while I have unconfessed sin within me. I cannot be filled with the Spirit while at the same time conducting my life in the energy of the flesh. I cannot be filled with the Spirit while I am resisting God's will and relying only on myself. I need to be sure that I have taken care of the sins that have emerged in my life, that I have not ignored the wrong that I have done before God and to others. I need to walk in conscious dependence on the Lord on a daily basis.

Many a morning I begin my day by sitting on the side of the bed, saying:

This is your day, Lord. I want to be at Your disposal. I have no idea what these next twenty-four hours will contain. But before I sip my first cup of coffee, and even before I get dressed, I want You to know that from this moment on throughout this day, I'm Yours, Lord. Help me to lean on You, to draw strength from You, and to have You fill my mind and my thoughts. Take control of my senses so that I am literally filled with Your presence and empowered with Your energy. I want to be Your tool, Your vessel today. I can't make it happen. And so I'm saying, Lord, fill me with Your Spirit today.

I challenge you to begin every day with a similar prayer. "Lord, today, enable me to live out the authentic Christian life for Your glory." Customize it with your own details depending on what may be the needs of that particular day.

2. Be filled with the Spirit.

It's hard to tell in English, but in the original Greek, it's easy to see this command is plural. In Texas we say, "y'all." As in, "All y'all be filled with the Spirit." It's for all of us. There's no unique group that qualifies to be filled. If you're a believer, you get fuel in your tank. You're able to drop your car into gear and drive. If you don't, it's your problem, not God's. The fuel is inside. You're engaging the gears.

We don't need to spend our days wondering why some people have an edge on the power. You and I have it too. We don't need to toss and turn through sleepless nights, struggling over our inability to claim the same super-dynamic power that some televangelist seems to have and we don't. Let me repeat: as a Christian you *have* the Spirit of God.

3. Be filled with the Spirit.

It's also given in a passive voice—grammatically that means something is done *to* us. You're not doing the filling; you have to *be* filled. One Bible translation says, "Let the Spirit fill your life" (CEV). He knows what you really need in the moment, so be at peace. Find your comfort, wisdom, and confidence in Him. He is able to bring you those things through the filling of His Spirit, but He's not a coercive God. He waits for you to ask Him: "Lord, I'm Yours today. Lord, I want to glorify You today. Please enable me to accomplish that. Fill me with Your power . . . strength . . . peace . . . love. I need You to do that."

4. Be filled with the Spirit.

It's in the present tense—literally "keep on being filled." It's not once in a lifetime or once every year; it's every so often. Get to the place where you are aware moment by moment of who is controlling you. Asking God to fill You with His Spirit is an essential part of walking by faith and not by sight.

Not too long ago I was facing a very difficult task. I remember driving in my truck to the destination where I'd be dealing with this hard issue, and all along the way I prayed out loud. No radio, no news, no music. Just peace and quiet. I said, "Lord, I'm not sure what I'm going to encounter here, and without Your help, I'll be in way over my head. Take over. Fill me with Your words. Give me the right response. Restrain any reaction that would be inappropriate. Speak through me with wisdom and with grace. Let me be Your voice in this situation."

You may be agreeing with me right now, saying, "Lord, I want to be filled by You. I want to be used by You." Two hours from now, you may need to pray that again. There's no singular moment where you experience the fullness of the Spirit and from then on you are on an all-time high that never wanes. This is by God's design. He wants us to be aware of our moment-by-moment dependence on Him. Instead, we are regularly to pray, "Fill me, Lord, for this moment . . . fill me in this hour . . . fill me as I'm facing this challenge. I want to be used. I want to be available. I deliberately make myself dependent upon You."

The Spirit's filling is like walking. When we were young—very young—every tiny step was a conscious effort and a magnificent achievement. Soon we learned to link two or three steps together before we fell. And then before you know it, we were walking and not even thinking about it. Walking has simply become a part of life.

Over time, as we experience His filling, it becomes a constant part of our consciousness and our life. But we begin deliberately, slowly, and carefully. We need the Lord to enable us with discernment, to walk in obedience, to sense wrong when we encounter it and stay away from it. To keep us strong when temptation comes. To guard our tongues from saying the wrong things or saying too much or speaking too quickly. We need the Spirit to take our eyes, take our tongues, take our emotions, take our wills and use us, because we want to operate under His control on a continuing basis.

This, my friend, is called the Christian walk.

How Will My Life Be Different When the Spirit Fills Me?

A wonderful thing about the Bible is that if you read it closely enough, you'll see that it answers many of its own questions. The question, "What is the result of being filled with the Spirit?" is answered in Ephesians 5:18–21:

> And do not get drunk with wine, for that is dissipation, but be filled with the Spirit, speaking to one another in psalms and hymns and spiritual songs, singing and making melody with your heart to the Lord; always giving thanks for all things in the name of our Lord Jesus Christ to God, even the Father; and be subject to one another in the fear of Christ.

WHEN I'M FILLED WITH THE SPIRIT . . .

Let's take a closer look at several important truths mentioned here.

When I'm filled with the Spirit, my heart is teachable.

Verse 19 mentions "speaking to one another." The Spirit's filling affects our speaking—that's the first result. When I'm filled with the Spirit, I'm able to share information that's helpful to other people. Hopefully that's happening right now. And you are, by being filled with the Spirit, open to the teaching. You're growing in Christ by learning this truth.

It also means I'm open to being admonished. Every once in a while, a good friend or my wife or one of my children will say, "There's something you need to know." And they'll bring up something that's been hurtful or difficult for them to deal with in me. When I'm filled with the Spirit, I'm open to that and I appreciate it. When I'm not filled with the Spirit, I'm closed off and I don't want to hear it. We have all experienced both sides of that situation, and so we understand that to speak to one another correctly and sensitively is easier when we are filled with the Spirit.

When I'm filled with the Spirit, my heart is melodious.

Life takes on a special lilt; joy returns when we are filled with the Spirit. I love the end of verse 19—"singing and making melody with your heart to the Lord"—because I love to sing. One of the characteristics of the filling of the Spirit is your heart becomes melodious. Chances are good if you don't enjoy music, it's because you can't carry a tune. But know this: when you sing to God, He never says, "Whoa, you're so off key." Instead He hears the inner melody of your heart. I hope you enjoy times when you just belt out your songs at the top of your lungs. (Preferably when you're all alone.)

The other day I was singing in the car and I hit a note I didn't even know I could hit anymore. I was glad no one was with me to say, "That sounded terrible. Pipe down, Swindoll." You know why my heart was melodious? Because I had seen something great in Scripture that only a song could express. That music came directly from the Spirit and it was a sweet moment between the Lord and me. Some translations say, "Sing heartily unto the Lord." *Heartily* is a good biblical word for that feeling when the Spirit's filling opens our hearts and moves us into an enthusiastic overflow of worship.

By the way, a melodious heart is never a grumbling heart . . .

When I'm filled with the Spirit, my heart is grateful.

Gratitude is an eloquent statement of the Spirit's filling. Verse 20 says, "always giving thanks for all things." Grumbling is a sure sign that the flesh in control. I'm not saying that you shouldn't live with your eyes open; of course you need discernment. But don't grumble. If the Spirit is in control, life doesn't get reduced to a bunch of gripes and grumbles. You're giving thanks—all the time.

Show me a grumbler, and I'll show you a person who has distanced herself or himself from the Spirit of God. When we are filled with the Spirit, there is an overwhelming sense of thankfulness. We are not hard to please. We are happy to have whatever God provides.

When I'm filled with the Spirit, my heart is humble.

Ephesians 5:21 is one of the most misapplied verses in Scripture: "And be subject to one another in the fear of Christ."

Even though some will accuse me of meddling, hear this well: there's no rank in the body of Christ. God calls for mutual submission one to another. Not only are you submissive to those in authority over you; those who are filled with the Spirit are submissive to you. All ground is level at the foot of the cross.

It may surprise some men that there's no gender mentioned in this command. This is important, especially for those men who *love* it when we get to the "Wives, be subject to your own husbands" line (v. 22). That's the way we tend to read it (wrongly). And we're quick to go, "Look at that, honey, that's right there in the Bible."

Several years ago I spoke at a Promise Keepers conference alongside a friend of mine, Jack Hayford. Jack is so much fun to be with. He told me a terrific story about a couple who went to a marriage conference. It so happened that one of the featured speakers hammered away at the topic of wives being submitted to their husbands. Well, that husband loved it. He drank it all in.

So when they get home, he slammed the door as they walked inside and she just looked at him. He swaggered, "I've been thinking about what that fellow said tonight, and I want you to know that from now on *that's* the way it's gonna be around here. You got it? *You* submit to *me*."

And having said that, he didn't see her for two weeks.

After three weeks, he could start to see her just a little bit out of one eye.

The Spirit-filled walk will not only change a life; in the process it absolutely transforms a home. Something is twisted in the mind of the man who thinks submission is limited to the woman. From experience I know that there is seldom a problem with submission in the home when a husband has a heart that is genuinely submissive to God. The reason is clear: with a heart submissive to God, the Spirit-filled man truly loves his wife as Christ loved the church . . . and there's no one else on earth he loves quite like her. He demonstrates it by listening when she speaks, by respecting her opinion, by caring for her, by releasing many of his own rights. Part of love is sharing. When a wife knows that she is enveloped in that kind of respectful attention, she has no trouble at all yielding to her husband.

Why would any husband strive to be like that? Ephesians 5:21 explains, "Be subject to one another in the fear of Christ." In other words, out of respect for Christ.

You know why I listen when my wife speaks? Because I respect Christ. You know why she listens to me when I say what may be hard for her to hear? Because she respects Christ. When both of you respect Christ, it does an amazing thing to your ability to communicate. The barriers just drop, and we're open to each other.

SOME PRACTICAL IMPLICATIONS

Let me wrap all this up with a couple of very practical comments, one regarding the church and the second regarding the world in which we live.

The Church

The church doesn't need monthly miracles; it needs daily enablement. Find a congregation enabled by the Spirit, and either become a part . . . or get out of their way. They're on the move. All they need is to be led in a direction and then for you to say "thank you." It's amazing how that happens. We need to be a collective body of individuals whose lives are unexplainable apart from the supernatural work of the Spirit—growing us, transforming us, loving us to good works, as we increasingly look like Christ.

The World

You want to make an impact on someone who has yet to receive Christ? Be real. They'll be disarmed most by your authenticity, not by some story of a miracle. People aren't looking for the amazing; they're looking for the authentic. "You're a real guy." "You really do trust the Lord." "You really do believe God's Word." "You really do care about me." If you will live with that kind of authenticity, they're going to want to know how you do it, because they can't seem to live like that. The only way to explain it is to point to the Spirit of God alive and in control in you.

Too often we've gone our own way and suffered the consequences. We've carried out what *we* wanted and we haven't done what *He's* wanted, and we grieve over that. Even more tragic, the Spirit grieves because He lives within us to take control.

May this day be different. Ask yourself three questions:

- Am I keeping short accounts on those things that break fellowship with God?

- Am I walking in conscious dependence on the Lord?

- Am I saying to Him at the beginning of—and frequently throughout—the day, "Lord, my life is Yours"?

∞ 4 ∞

HOW DO I KNOW
I'M LED BY THE SPIRIT?

A slammed door is a harsh sound. It's hard to hear . . .
and even harder to experience, especially if you have
prayed, genuinely asking the Lord to lead you.

You've waited, you've sought the counsel of people
you admire, you've studied sections of His Word that
might very well lead you into the way you ought to go,
you've spent time alone weighing the pros and cons. You
have continued to pray, your heart is willing, your spirit
is ready, your soul is soaring. And about the time you get
near it, *bang!* . . . the door slams shut.

Up until now, our study of God's Spirit has been
fairly safe. Now it gets extremely personal and complex.
In fact, this topic of "how God's Spirit leads us" might
dig up questions from past experiences that have spent
years unanswered or perhaps open up an old wound in
your spirit. Or it may speak to something you're dealing
with today as you seek God's direction on an important

decision. If any of this is the case, then I hope you will get much-needed insight that will guide you to the other side of those issues. Keep an open mind. Allow the Lord to lead you into His truth on this personal matter of how He directs our lives.

When you love the Lord, you sincerely want the direction of your life to be in harmony with God's will. Deep within, we all wish His specific directives would be spelled out in the Scriptures. Wouldn't it be a relief to take God by His powerful hand and let Him escort you where He wants you to go? None of us wants to miss God's best for our lives. We want to be held on a steady course by His guiding presence.

So where do we find that direction, that leading? This is the work of the Holy Spirit, the Helper who comes alongside us.

If we could see the Spirit at work in our lives, we would realize that in every situation God is doing hundreds of things we cannot see and do not know. He is at work, as silent as light in some situations and as obvious as a truck in others. In both cases, He provides us with exactly what we need to face whatever lies ahead.

In place of weakness, the Spirit brings power.

In place of ignorance, He brings knowledge.

In place of human knowledge, He delivers divine wisdom and profound insights from the depths of God's sovereign plan.

As we grasp these depths, we gain confidence in His direction.

And when God's leading is clear, there is only one option: *obedience.*

The One Who Comes Alongside

The Spirit of God wants to help us. He's not hiding any of the pearls of His promises or the gems of His wisdom. God wants us to know His will so we can walk in it and experience the benefits of His power and blessings.

Let's return again to the final hours Jesus had with the disciples as He explained the Spirit's future role in their lives: "But the Helper, the Holy Spirit, whom the Father will send in My name, *He will teach you all things,* and *bring to your remembrance all that I said to you*" (John 14:26, emphasis mine). Twice Jesus used the term *helper. Helper* is translated into English from a combination of two Greek terms: *para* ("alongside") and *kaleo* ("to call"). The Holy Spirit is the One whom our Lord will "call alongside" for the purpose of giving us help—specifically in two ways:

1. The Spirit will teach you "all things."
2. The Spirit will "bring to your remembrance" what Jesus said.

In other words, it is the Lord's desire to *reveal* truth rather than hide it. He wants to help us *remember* rather than forget. It's the Spirit's job to remind us of what is true and trustworthy. Jesus assures us that the Spirit will do for us what we cannot do for ourselves. God promises to "guide you into all the truth" (John 16: 13). Imagine!

Can you recall struggling with a decision? The more you wrestled, the greater the confusion. In the beginning you felt as if you were standing in a thick, dark cloud. Then, gradually, the fog lifted and you could see your way through. That, I believe, can be traced to the Spirit's work of revealing truth to us.

I can think of several surprising moments when I have been the recipient of the Spirit's disclosures.

- Biblical insights I would otherwise have missed.
- A sudden awareness of God's will or the presence of danger or a sense of peace in the midst of chaos.
- A surge of bold confidence in a setting where there would otherwise have been fear and hesitation.
- A quiet, calm awareness that I was not alone, even though no other person was actually with me.
- The undeniable, surrounding awareness of evil . . . including the dark sinister presence of demonic forces.

In each case I was made aware of the truth, which the Spirit disclosed to me.

Prerequisites to the Spirit's Leading

How does this happen? Some essential basics must be in place before we can expect the Holy Spirit's guidance. These are a must!

First and foremost, you must be a Christian.

> For all who are being led by the Spirit of God, these are sons of God. (Rom. 8:14)

When you accept Christ as the Savior and Master of your life, the Holy Spirit comes to live within you. Among other things, He is there to reveal to you how you should live. Only the believer has the Spirit's presence within. This inside help is essential if we are ever going to follow Him.

When the Lord provided your salvation at conversion, His Spirit came within you as part of the initial package deal. Without your knowing it, the Spirit of God took up permanent residence within you. When He entered your life, He brought you the full capacity of His power. Without Christ, you and I are like a vast, empty reservoir awaiting the coming of a downpour. When salvation became a reality, this emptiness filled to the point of running over. The Spirit of God filled our internal capacity with power and dynamic force.

For some of you, the Spirit is leading you right now and for the first time to the cross, where Jesus Christ died, paying the full penalty for your sin. His blood, the greatest detergent in the history of time, sufficient to wash away all of your sins, was poured out for you. Today, perhaps for the first time, you understand your need. You now realize God's provision of life and salvation.

If so, right now, turn your life over to Christ. Pray these simple words: "Lord, I don't know quite how to put this, but I know I'm a sinner, and I know You're holy, and I know there's a big distance between You and me. But today, for the first time in my life, I take Your Son as my Savior and Lord. I believe in Him now. I repent of my sin. I take the gift that You're offering me. Thank You for forgiving me my sins. I put my life in Your hands."

If this decision is yours today, I want to help you get started on this new and wonderful life. Please call or write Insight for Living and tell someone about your decision. You'll find our contact information in the back of this book.

Second, you must be wise.

> Therefore be careful how you walk, not as unwise men but as wise, making the most of your time, because the days are evil. (Eph. 5:15–16)

Pure foolishness can occur when people attempt to decipher God's leading in the wrong way. Refrain from all extremes. Don't start looking for the face of Jesus in an enchilada. Don't start thinking that some cloud formation represents the Last Supper. God tells us not to be foolish, but wise, making the most of our time, taking every opportunity that comes our way and using it wisely.

Following the will of God requires wisdom—the art of skillful living, and, yes, some good old garden-variety common sense. Such a mixture also helps us understand God's direction.

Third, you must really want *to follow the Lord's leading.*

> If anyone is willing to do His will, he shall know of the teaching, whether it is of God or whether I speak from Myself. (John 7:17)

You really want to do what He wants you to do . . . more than anything else. More than completing your education, more than getting married, more than getting out of debt—more than anything else you want to do the will of God.

Looking back on my own life, I know there were times I said I wanted the Spirit to lead me but I really didn't. That's a tough thing to confess, but with 20/20 hindsight, I realize that on occasion I resisted following. I've learned that serious consequences follow selfish ambitions.

Ephesians 6:6 describes this desire as "doing the will of God *from the heart*" (emphasis mine). Following God from the heart—that's as deep as it gets. More than pleasing people, more than staying comfortable and safe, you want to please God. No matter where He may lead, you want to follow.

Fourth, you must be willing to pray and to wait.

> This is the confidence which we have before Him, that, if we ask anything according to His will, He hears us. And if we know that He hears us in whatever we ask, we know that we have the requests which we have asked from Him. (1 John 5:14–15)

There are times when knowing and then following the will of God can be a lengthy and painful process. Back in the early 1990s both the president and the chairman of the board of Dallas Theological Seminary asked me to consider becoming the next president of that school. For more than twenty years I had been the pastor of a church in Fullerton, California. I was not looking for a change, nor did I feel any urgent "push" to entertain their offer. In fact, I spent only a small amount of time in prayer and discussion with my wife before I wrote a letter to the president and the chairman, stating that I had no sense of God's leading me in that direction.

As I recall, I listed several "airtight" reasons I should not make such a change in my calling. All of these reasons made good sense, which led me to believe I should not consider the issue any further. I wrote a convincing two-page letter that made sense logically . . . but it was wrong!

The Spirit of God would not leave me alone. In subtle yet definite ways He kept bringing the thought back to my mind. I'd shove it aside, only to have Him resurface it. I would ignore the prompting within, but He would not allow me to go very long without another thought returning, prodding me to reconsider. A painful struggle followed.

In the meantime, several other events transpired, forcing me to return to the subject. God was going to have His way, whether I was open or not! He refused to leave me alone. There were other phone calls, visits, protracted times spent alone in prayer and with the Scriptures, lengthy conversations with those I respected, and numerous restless nights. Finally, my heart was turned in that direction and I found myself unable to resist any longer. By the end of 1993, I had come full circle: it was the Lord's leading. I could resist it no longer. Surprised and amazed, I said yes. A remarkable sense of inner peace brought relief to my soul.

So, then, how does God lead us into His will today? Without removing all the mystery that often accompanies

His will, I have discovered several absolutes that assist us in following the Lord.

How Does God Lead Today?

I could probably list at least ten ways that God leads His children today, but I will limit myself to the four that I think are His most significant methods.

First and most basic, God leads us through His written Word.

> Your word is a lamp to my feet and a light to my path. (Ps. 119:105)

While our individual experiences may vary as to how the Lord directs us in unique ways, you must never—and I mean never—get too far from the revealed and reliable Word of God. If you do, you will begin to use your experience as a basis for your beliefs, and the Scriptures will diminish in importance as you make more and more room for more strange experiences.

Stay with the Scriptures. As long as you keep the plumb line true, just remember that you may have a great deal of space between where you are and where the Spirit wants you to be.

Second, God leads us through the inner prompting of the Holy Spirit.

I will instruct you and teach you in the way which you should go; I will counsel you with My eye upon you. (Ps. 32:8)

The Spirit of God is at work within, steering us. That inner prompting is crucial, because much of the time we can't imagine the next step. "Man's steps are ordained by the LORD, how then can man understand his way?" (Prov. 20:24). I love that! When all is said and done, you'll say, "Honestly, I didn't figure this thing out on my own; it must have been God." The longer I live the Christian life, the less I know about why He leads as He does. In addition, I can't figure out His timing. But I do know that He leads.

Nothing wrong with planning. Nothing wrong with thinking it through. Nothing wrong with doing your charts, listing all the pros and cons. Nothing wrong with talking it over. But as you are moving along, stay sensitive to the quiet, yet all-important, prompting of God through His Holy Spirit. It's easier to steer a moving car. Get the car rolling and you can push it into the service station to get the gas. Just stay open. By doing so, you may well sense inner promptings that will spur a thought such as, *I can't believe I'm still interested in that. I wonder what the Lord is up to. I wonder where He's going with this.*

"Watch to see where God is at work and join Him!" says author Henry Blackaby. "Go where God is." Why do you want to be anywhere God isn't at work?

Third, God leads us through the counsel of wise, qualified, trustworthy people.

This does not mean some maharishi in Tibet or serious-looking stranger at the bus stop. Ask for counsel from someone who has proven himself or herself wise and trustworthy and is therefore qualified to advise on a given matter. Usually such individuals are older and more mature than we are. Furthermore, they have nothing to gain or lose. This also means that they are not in our immediate family or our close friends or serving on the same staff. (These usually have too much vested interest to give objective help.)

At critical moments in my own life, I have sought the counsel of seasoned individuals—and they've seldom been wrong. But you must choose your counselors very carefully. Wise and trustworthy counselors are persons who want for you only what God wants. Such persons will stay objective, listen carefully, think deeply, and answer slowly.

Finally, the Holy Spirit leads us into His will by giving us an inner assurance of peace.

Let the peace of Christ rule in your hearts [Paul
wrote to the Colossians], to which indeed you were
called in one body; and be thankful. (Col. 3:15)

God's inner assurance of peace will act as an umpire in
your heart. Although peace is an emotion, I have found it
wonderfully reassuring as I've wrestled with following the
Lord's direction. This God-given calm comes in spite of
the obstacles or the odds, regardless of the risk or danger.
It's almost like God's way of saying, "I'm in this decision
. . . trust Me through it." I've heard it said that emotion
makes a lousy engine—driving the decision—but it is a
great caboose, coming along at the end.

FOLLOWING GOD IN THE REAL WORLD

Following the Spirit's leading is reality, not theory. We
have discussed some of the prerequisites and requirements for following the Spirit's lead; now comes the
bottom line: we have to do it in the real world. Again,
Henry Blackaby gives some good advice about following
the Spirit's lead in his fine book *Experiencing God*. He
said it almost always begins with a "crisis of belief." Following God's leading will demand a change. You cannot
continue life as usual or stay where you are and go with

God at the same time. Faith and action are like twins; they go together.

Imagine how hard it must have been for Moses to combine faith and action when he took that first step into the Red Sea. And as he did, God opened up a dry path through the sea.

Imagine the step of faith Noah took in quitting his job and building an ark.

Jonah had to leave his home and overcome a major prejudice in order to preach in Nineveh.

The disciples Peter, Andrew, James, and John had to walk away from their fishing businesses to follow Jesus.

The list of examples is long. In every generation, the people who wanted to follow God went through major crises of faith and adjustment.

Blackaby wrote:

> The kind of assignments God gives in the Bible are always God sized. They are always beyond what people can do because He wants to demonstrate His nature, His strength, His provision, His kindness to His people and to a watching world. That is the only way the world will come to know Him.[1]

Hebrews 11:6 tells us that "without faith it is impossible to please Him, for he who comes to God must believe that He is and that He is a rewarder of those who seek Him." Following Christ means that we must believe God is who He says He is and He will do what He says He will do. That sounds so elementary, but it has profound ramifications.

When Cynthia and I started *Insight for Living* back in 1979, we were total novices. We had no background in radio, no understanding of the world of media, and virtually no money to buy air time. We rarely listened to Christian radio. But that was where the Lord's God-sized plan took us. For over three uninterrupted decades, we have had to believe that God is who He says He is and will do what He says He will do. At times we've been backed into a corner, with seemingly no way out, and have been forced to trust Him. Invariably, He will move in a special way to give us direction. When it comes time to roll the credits, His name is the only One that deserves to be listed.

LET'S MAKE THIS PERSONAL

Question 1: What makes following Christ difficult for you?
Walking with the Lord is a risky path, and when we live and lean on our own understanding, everything within us screams, "Just leave it alone. If it ain't broke, don't fix it." But sometimes things need to be rearranged even

though they aren't broken. Sometimes we need a major change of direction—not necessarily because we are going in the wrong direction, but perhaps because it's just not the direction God wants for us. God does not want us to substitute the good for the very best.

Question 2: Are you willing to make a major change in your life—assuming that the Lord is leading?
I'm now convinced that much of what we wrestle with is less "What does the Lord want me to do?" and more "Am I willing to do it, once He makes it clear?"

Question 3: Have you ever followed what you thought was God's leading, only to have those plans fall apart?
We're back to where we were at the beginning of this chapter: open doors versus closed doors. What did you do when you thought you were following God's lead and everything was going along great . . . until it wasn't? I'd like to camp here for the rest of the chapter because I know as a pastor that this is where many people are living.

I want to tell you first that Cynthia and I have encountered a few closed doors that to this day we still cannot explain. Like you, we sought to do what we believed to be God's direction with all our hearts. We asked for guidance, we laid ourselves before Him, we held nothing tightly, willing to give up whatever needed to be given up to make it happen. *Bang!* There it would be again: a closed door.

Perhaps you can identify.

You envisioned a great business and so you moved from a familiar field of work to an unfamiliar area. There seemed to be every reason to make that move. Opportunities opened. You stepped into the new work, and it wasn't long before you realized . . . it just wasn't right for you.

You cultivated a relationship with a fine person and you spent months, perhaps years, really getting to know one another and in the process you fell deeply in love. Just as you got to the subject of marriage, *bang!* . . . the door slammed, the romance cooled, and the relationship ended. Closed door.

You were in a ministry. You were pouring your life into it, excited to be used by God. Then something changed—in the organization, in the demands, in your perspective—and suddenly the fruitful season ended. What happened?

You got your heart set on a particular school. You had the grades and a good résumé. But they could only take so many applicants, and when the final cut came, *bang!* . . . you weren't chosen. No explanation, no reason. You became disillusioned. The door had closed. Period. End of story.

Or was it?

Dr. Bruce Waltke, one of my mentors in my study of Hebrew at seminary, used to say, "The longer I live and the closer I walk with Christ, the more I believe He does not take the time to explain why. So we trust Him through our lives without expecting the 'why' to be answered."

You don't live very long in the Christian life before you realize that closed doors and open doors happen regularly . . . but they are often surprising. As profoundly as we may pray and as consistently as we may make ourselves available to follow the Lord's leading, there are times that His answer is "not this way." That's right . . . "no." Closed door.

It's our tendency, being only human, to use a little force when we encounter a closed door. After all, we've worked pretty hard for this plan. I mean, we gave up what we had over there and we moved over here, and we're not going to take a closed door sitting down. So we get out the crowbar of ingenuity, or we use some carnal creativity, and we start working on the door, because we're gonna pry that door open.

Stop . . . stop. Take it from one who's done that too many times. Anytime you force a door, thinking you'll find satisfaction by getting your way, ultimately you will regret it. Leave it closed. Back away. Accept it. In acceptance lies peace.

A Classic Example

In Acts 16 we find an example of how a closed door slammed in the faces of some of God's true servants. Two missionaries, Paul and Silas, and their young protégé Timothy were on their way across Turkey, which is called Asia in this biblical account. As they traveled they ministered at the young churches along the way. "The churches were being strengthened in the faith, and were increasing in number daily" (16:5). This was a pagan and idolatrous country; yet all across the area, people were coming to Christ, and churches were being founded.

Next, they left the familiar area and moved on toward the Galatian region with high hopes. Read about what happened: "They passed through the Phrygian and Galatian region, *having been forbidden by the Holy Spirit to speak the word in Asia*; and after they came to Mysia, they were trying to go into Bithynia, and *the Spirit of Jesus did not permit them*" (16:6–7, emphasis mine).

Bang! One closed door followed another.

Wait! They'd *had* an open door. All the lights were *green*. But as they got closer to the more central and southern regions, God closed the door. "The Spirit of Jesus did not permit them."

So they thought, *Obviously the Lord is leading another way.* And so "when they had come to Mysia, they were trying to go into Bithynia."

Let's use our own geography to get a better sense of their journey. They started in South Carolina, made their way over into Tennessee, and the door closed. So they went down to Alabama, Mississippi, and Louisiana. "Maybe we can preach there." Nope, another closed door. "Well, let's go up to Kansas and on into Nebraska. How about North Dakota?" *Slam, slam . . .* closed door. One closed door after another after another.

So they wound up at Troas. That's like trudging all the way to Oregon. Go any further and you'll walk right into the ocean. Likewise in Turkey, you can't go further than Troas. It's the northwestern-most point of the continent.

As they looked at the ocean, Paul must have thought, *Lord, I don't get it.* He, Timothy, and Silas must have sought the Lord for hours, asking, "What are You trying to do, God? What are You trying to tell us? Why all the closed doors? Look at the people we've left unevangelized! You've not allowed us to speak one word to them!"

Our tendency is to jump ahead to the amazing message Paul got next. But pause long enough to enter into their disappointment and frustration for a moment. They couldn't preach in either Phrygia or Galatia, nor were they permitted to share Christ in Mysia or Bithynia. Forbidden by the Lord! They had to pass through those populated places where the good news was sorely needed and yet be quiet! They had to travel as far away as they could—all the way to Troas. It made no sense.

You've been in that kind of situation, haven't you? This looked like what you ought to do, and you threw yourself into it, and you invested in it, whether it was time or money or gifts or effort, and *bang!* . . . to your shock, the door slammed shut. It's always difficult to know why.

I don't know how long Paul was in Troas, waiting and praying, but one night everything changed.

A vision appeared to him in the night: "A man of Macedonia was standing and appealing to him, and saying, 'Come over to Macedonia and help us'" (Acts 16:9).

Some people read this and think, *That's what I need, a night vision.* No, you don't. It's not dreams and visions we need in order to follow the Spirit. But in those days before the Scriptures were completed Paul needed a phenomenal, Spirit-guided evidence of what God wanted him to do.

That man in Macedonia said, "Come over and help us." In other words, he urged them to sail the northern waters of the Aegean Sea, travel across an entire continent to another culture and another language. Closed door on one side; open door on the other. Thankfully Paul was ready and willing. When he got the word, they took the first ship out of port and "immediately we sought to go into Macedonia, concluding that God had called us to preach the gospel to them" (Acts 16:10).

Look what God had waiting for them there:

> We were staying in this city for some days. And on the Sabbath day we went outside the gate to a riverside, where we were supposing that there would be a place of prayer; and we sat down and began speaking to the women who had assembled. A woman named Lydia, from the city of Thyatira, a seller of purple fabrics, a worshiper of God, was listening; and the Lord opened her heart to respond to the things spoken by Paul. (Acts 16:12–14)

This is the first work of evangelism in Europe recorded in the New Testament. This was the seed of the church at Philippi, the church at Thessalonica, and the church at Corinth. God was already at work. He had closed the door to Turkey without asking permission, without warning, and without any explanation, yet the door now swung wide open in Europe. Hearts were ready for the sowing of the seed.

CLOSED AND OPEN DOORS STILL HAPPEN

Several years ago I was asked to speak at an anniversary reunion of the Navigators at Estes Park, Colorado. At the end of the week, one of the men drove me back to Denver so I could catch my plane. On the way he said, "Can I tell you my story?"

"Sure," I said.

"Actually, it's a story of closed doors and open doors."

"Great," I said, "I've had a few of those, so tell me what yours were."

"Well," he began, "my wife and I could not find peace, in any manner, staying in the States. While at a conference years ago with a number of the leaders of the Navigators, I was offered the opportunity to open our work in Uganda.

"Uganda?" he said. "I could hardly spell it when they pointed to it on the map and said, 'Perhaps that's where the Lord would have you and your family go.'

"I went home, I told my wife and our three children about it, and we began to pray." He said to his wife, "Honey, are you ready to take on the challenge of Uganda?"

And she said, "If that's the door God has opened for us, I'm ready for the challenge." Wonderful response.

So they flew to Nairobi, Kenya, where he put his family up in a hotel while he rented a Land Rover and drove across the border into Uganda to check out the situation. It was just after Idi Amin's reign of terror.

"One of the first things that caught my eye when I came into the village where I was going to spend my first night were several young kids with automatic weapons, shooting them off into the sky. As I drove by, they stared at me and pointed their guns." Nothing happened, but it was that kind of volatile setting. He thought, *Lord, are You in this?* His heart sank as night fell.

By now the streets were dark. He pulled up to a dingy, dimly lit hotel. Inside, he went up to the registration counter. The clerk, who spoke only a little English, told him there was one bed available. So he walked up two flights of stairs and opened the door and turned on the light—a naked light bulb hanging over a table. He saw a room with two beds, one unmade and one still made up. He immediately realized, "I am sharing this room with somebody else." A chill went down his spine.

That did it. He needed the kind of encouragement only God could provide. "I dropped to my knees and I said, 'Lord, look, I'm afraid. I'm in a country I don't know, in a culture that's totally unfamiliar. I have no idea who sleeps in that bed. Please, show me You're in this move!'"

And then, he said, "Just as I was finishing my prayer, the door flung open and there stood this six-foot five-inch African frowning at me, saying in beautiful British English, 'What are you doing in my room?'

"I stood there for a moment, and then I muttered, 'They gave me this bed, but I'll only be here one night.'"

"What are you doing in my country?" the African asked.

"Well, I'm with a little organization called the Navigators."

"Ahh! The Navigators!" Suddenly the tall African broke into an enormous grin, threw his arms around his new roommate, and laughed out loud.

"He lifted me up off the floor and just danced around the room with me."

"Praise God, praise God," said this African.

Finally they sat down at the table, and this brother in Christ said, "For two years I have prayed that God would send someone to me from this organization." And he pulled out a little Scripture memory-verse pack and pointed to where, at the bottom of each of the verses, it read, "The Navigators, Colorado Springs, Colorado."

"Are you from Colorado Springs, Colorado?" he asked.

"I was. But I'm coming to Uganda to begin a work for the Navigators in this country."

The door of new hope flew open in my friend's life. That African was from Uganda. He became a member

of the board for his ministry . . . He helped him find
a place to live . . . He taught him all about the culture
. . . He assisted him with the language and became his
best friend for the many years they were there, serving
Christ.

Doors are closed. Doors are opened. Lives are
changed.

FOUR GUIDELINES THAT WILL HELP

If you're struggling with a closed door, I have four guide-
lines to share with you that have helped me in my own
process.

1. Since God is sovereign, He is in full control.

Read Revelation 3:7: "[I am the One] who opens and no
one will shut, and who shuts and no one opens."

*2. Being in full control, God takes full responsibility for
the results.*

Don't try to carry that burden. It's not up to you to make
the divine plan work; it's up to God. Your job is to walk
in His will, regardless; it's God's job to make everything
come together.

*3. The closing of a good opportunity occurs in order to lead
you to a better one.*

Often in the winds of change we find a new direction. Consider the story you just read. A good door closed in the States for that dear family; a better door opened in Uganda.

I've heard countless stories like this through many years of ministry. "I got to the end of my rope, I tied a knot and hung on. I trusted the Lord through this, and you can't believe what opened as a result of my not pushing my way in the direction I thought I was supposed to go." God took over and turned a jolt into joy.

4. Not until we walk through the open door will we realize the necessity of the previously closed one.

As a result of obeying God, accepting the closed doors, and walking through the open ones, God will honor you with a perspective you would never otherwise have. Henri Nouwen wrote, "The years that lie behind you, with all their struggles and pains, will in time be remembered only as the way that led to your new life."[2]

Let's go back to my Uganda story. After more than a dozen years, the Navigator work was well established and my friend's job in Uganda was finished. Another person from the staff of the Navigators picked up the mantle as my friend and his family returned to the States. They had been back not quite a year when his son's high school class went to Washington, DC, for their senior field trip. The father said to his boy, "Son, here's forty dollars. Buy something for yourself that will be a great memory of your trip to our nation's capital."

His son left for several days. When he got back, he had a package with him. He said, "I want to surprise you, Dad."

So my friend waited until his son called him into his bedroom. As he walked into the room, he saw, hanging over the bed, a huge Ugandan flag.

"This is what I bought with the money you gave me," said the boy. "Those years in Uganda were the best years of my life, Dad."

Talk about perspective. The man feared that going to Uganda might hurt or hinder his family, when, in fact, his son now had an abiding passion for God's work outside the borders of the United States. It was a passion he would never have had if his father had not obeyed and walked through the open door.

Perhaps you've come to a closed door, and you've been resisting it, you've been pushing it, you've been fighting it. You've looked for someone to blame. It's hard for you to accept the fact that the door is truly closed. You've come to your own Bithynia or Mysia, and to your shock the door has closed. Ask the Lord to meet with you at your own personal Troas as you look out across that vast sea of possibilities. Ask Him to give you peace in a whole new direction. Like Paul at Troas, be open, be willing.

It is easy to become disillusioned and discouraged thinking we have missed His direction, when, in fact, we are in the very nucleus of His will. It is hard to have dreams dashed, to have hopes unfulfilled, to face a future that is unknown and unfamiliar and sometimes, if the truth were known, unwanted. But God has a way of guiding us unerringly into the path of righteousness for His name's sake.

Accept this closed door, give up the fight, let it be, my friend . . . let it be. You'll exchange a lot of intensity and worry for tranquility and relief. Let it go . . . and let the Spirit lead.

One More Essential: Take Time to Listen.

Do you want to follow God's Spirit's direction? Do you want to hear His voice . . . giving comfort, pointing direction, stirring faith in you? Do you want to be embraced by His Spirit?

Then you must spend time with Him. Important things seldom come on the run. You must keep your appointments with Him or you won't hear what He has to say to you. You won't know about His promises. You won't have much assurance about tomorrow.

It seems like we're always on a fast pace to somewhere. We're driving faster, we're walking faster, we're thinking faster. It's easy in our frenetic culture to forget the value of being still and learning that God is God. It's easier to worry and fear than remember that God's Spirit is with us and that He has promised to strengthen and stabilize us for every good work. When I pause and spend time in silence before the Lord, the slower pace helps peel off the veneer. The discipline of silence increases my sensitivity and decreases my anxiety.

I can say from experience that when I spend time with the Lord, I get fresh and creative thoughts. I get new ideas. I get directions. He stirs up my emotion. He gives me an urge in a specific area of my life. Yes, it's risky to walk with Him; it means I must be willing to hear what God is saying and to follow His plan. But the rewards of being embraced by His Spirit are countless and endless.

I would venture to say that some of you think you're in the center of God's leading right now, but when you begin to spend time with Him, you'll discover areas that God wants to fine tune. If you keep running you'll be too busy to notice that. I urge you—step out of the traffic and rest awhile.

If you want to follow God's lead . . . if you want to hear His Spirit's voice . . . if you want to know the confidence and security that come with the embrace of His Spirit, get closer and listen better. Ask Him to soften the soil of your heart that has been hardened by bitterness or sadness or resentment or blame because of previously closed doors. Ask God to create in you a spirit of willingness and availability. You will soon discover in the process a sweetness of relationship and a depth of intimacy with Him like you've never known before.

≈ 5 ≈

HOW DOES THE SPIRIT
FREE ME FROM SIN?

It is not a message we hear very often. Feel-good preachers avoid it like the plague. Most pastors would rather preach about anything else. I'm referring to our daily battle with sin. You're in the battle. I'm in the battle. It's relentless.

Sin in all its ugliness has a grip on us that we cannot escape, enslaving us in thought patterns and behaviors that grieve the Lord and hurt us. Without the Spirit's indwelling and constant help, sin would wrap its customized, personalized chains around us. It would destroy us . . . in a flash. As it is, sin's devastating effect on our personal lives is beyond what any of us would imagine. Up close, you and I have all felt the wretchedness of the battle, especially the battles we've lost.

A glance at today's news can convince us quickly enough that our world is in a death grip—held captive by sin. It's the ugly drive behind . . .

- deception at every level
- addictions of every kind
- abuse of our innocent
- the "me first" attitude pervasive in our homes, our workplaces, our churches that tears us apart from the inside
- all the things that make us selfish, unkind, impatient, angry, revengeful, greedy, and proud

That's our dreadful dark side.

We've also seen the beauty of the Holy Spirit's work in our lives conquering this perpetual enemy. Like a beacon of light, the Spirit can flood our lives with grace and relief. If you've been filled with the Spirit, as I've written about previously, you've known the joy He pours into our hearts and the refreshment He pours over us. You've experienced the power He enables us to have, setting us free, first from the penalty of sin, and then from its enslavement. This freedom is where we want to go in this chapter . . . but we must first lay the foundation.

VICTORY'S BATTLE PLAN

Romans chapters 6, 7, and 8 set forth our battle strategy in broad strokes. Let's start with our problem and then turn to the solution.

Romans 6

Good news: because of Christ's work on our behalf and the indwelling Spirit's power, sin no longer has control of us like it once did. We have been emancipated. The freedom is ours to claim. Our old way of life was nailed to the cross with Christ, putting a decisive end to that sin-miserable life. We're no longer at sin's every beck and call!

The liberating message of Romans 6 is encapsulated in verses 12–13: "Therefore do not let sin reign in your mortal body so that you obey its lusts, and do not go on presenting the members of your body to sin as instruments of unrighteousness; but present yourselves to God." "You're free from your old master," the apostle Paul wrote. "Don't let it reign over you any longer."

Romans 7

Bad news: you and I still battle with sin! We struggle over who is going to be in charge. We may have been freed, but the old master is still alive and well. Our struggle in so many words is, "I'm full of myself—after all, I've spent a long time in sin's prison. What I don't understand about myself is that I decide one way, but then I act another, doing things I absolutely despise" (Rom. 7:14–15 MSG).

The battle we fight with sin conveys a convoluted reality to those who watch us and live with us and are influenced by us. This is the confusing, frustrating struggle for every earthly follower of Christ. It won't change until He removes us from this planet.

In verse 18, I despair. "I know that nothing good dwells in me."

In verse 23, I'm in a battle. "A different law in the members of my body, waging war against the law of my mind and making me a prisoner of the law of sin which is in my members." It happens so regularly that it's predictable. The moment I decide to do good, sin is there to trip me up.

In verse 24, I see myself for who I am: "Wretched!"

That explains why a man who could help so many others would in a rash moment of decision hang himself. That explains why a pastor who for years preaches the glorious news of Jesus Christ can tumble and fall into a moral tailspin that ruins his reputation and steals the whole community's trust in him. "How on earth could a man do such a thing?" we ask. It's because he's "wretched." It's because the flesh won that war.

And before you allow yourself five seconds of judgment against anyone else, realize you have the same ugly potential within yourself. You have the same dark nature. It's no better in one than in another.

In verse 24, I'm trapped. I've tried everything and nothing helps. "Who will set me free from the body of this death?"

This heavy, dark seventh chapter in Romans describes what it feels like to be "condemned." Our sin condemns us. How? First comes guilt. Then shame accompanies it. Disappointment with ourselves follows. A low-grade depression lingers over the fact that we rebel against what we know to be right . . . even though we have within us the power to overcome it. No wonder we're exasperated! We have all been there. We've found ourselves reaping what we have sown in the flesh, and the consequences are, well, *wretched.*

Written across this chapter are the feelings of a tired man. He is exhausted from allowing that sin cycle to continue. "I'm a weary, wretched man. I feel hopeless. Who will deliver me? I'm condemned in this body of death. I'm trapped; who will set me free? "

Great question! Who indeed is able to give us the victory over our old master? Who indeed will "set me free" from the clawing, clutching, clinging presence of sin? We desperately need help; we're condemned on our own.

Chapter after chapter, the book of Romans deals with sin, sin, and more sin . . . with not one word of relief from the dark side. And then, as the curtain seems to close and the reader reaches rock bottom with no way through and no way out . . . *eureka!* Enter the Spirit of life. The curtain quickly reopens, the stage is flooded with light, and we're back to the same magnificent solution: the

Transformer Himself—the Holy Spirit! Which becomes the subject of . . .

Romans 8

Victorious news: the Spirit provides a new dimension of living. The depressing syndrome set forth in Romans 7 is overcome in Romans 8. The "law of sin and of death" that habitually condemned us in our lost estate has been conquered by "the Spirit of life in Christ Jesus" (v. 2). That is why "there is now no condemnation for those who are in Christ Jesus" (v. 1).

The whole emphasis of Romans 8 is our security in Christ. It starts with "No condemnation" and ends with "No separation." Verse 35 reads, "Who will separate us from the love of Christ?" Remember, this is just a short distance away from, "Wretched man that I am." Chapter 8 is like a grand crescendo that rises in dramatic emphasis toward your security in Christ. You cannot ever—no matter what—be separated from the love of God which is in Christ Jesus our Lord. What reassurance!

A NEW WAY OF LIVING

There is no way that I can exaggerate either the reality of sin or the relief brought by the Spirit. The best way I can think of is to take you to far west Texas. Picture yourself on a butte. You can see for miles—nothing but flat, barren, brown wilderness. The land is drought-scorched and desolate. The hot wind blows endlessly. If you're traveling by car, the miles are marked by endless monotony. Just sheer endurance keeps you at the wheel until you get to the far side of the panhandle and on up into the northern part of New Mexico.

There the landscape slowly begins to change as you rise through the Raton Pass that stands guard at the foot of the historic Santa Fe Trail. The pass climbs up, up, up to seven thousand feet till you get to the eastern side of the Sangre de Cristo Mountains on the Colorado border. Within moments the landscape takes on a new color—and it's green!

Ultimately you keep climbing, up through south and central Colorado till you get to the Rockies. Is there a more magnificent visual feast than the majestic Rockies of Colorado? Snowcapped peaks followed by more peaks defy description. They are stupendous!

That is what it is like to go from the barrenness of living in the flesh and travel into the beauty and magnificence of the power of the Holy Spirit. The Spirit takes over, occupies, and ultimately preoccupies your mind, lifting the monotony and the barrenness of days lived under the dark and dismal power of sin.

As God works within us and begins to break us free

from the consequences of sin and deliver us in such a marvelous way, He introduces a rush of cool breeze and the freshness of the green fruitfulness. His Spirit's life in us changes everything, refreshing and renewing us. Discouragement and despair are pushed aside as He rescues us, reminding us that He is at work within us.

Who would want to live any other way?

But truth be told, many people—perhaps you—still live on the desert floor. You live in fear of the old nature within you, still seeing yourself a helpless victim with no control over it. Still saying, "Well, I guess that's just the way I am." Still wandering, still wayward, still giving in to the power that has no rightful control over you. You're still living in the monotonous, barren wilderness. But it doesn't have to be that way. The Spirit invites you up, up, up to soaring heights.

OUR EMANCIPATION PROCLAMATION

Let's turn our thoughts now to the "how"—how does the Spirit set us free on a daily basis?

We can live our lives thinking that we have figured it out, only to discover later there's a whole other world going on that we missed in the process. I want to introduce to you an awareness that many (I'm tempted to say *most*) Christians do not have.

I'm referring to slavery. That may surprise you. Most of us have never witnessed firsthand the raw reality of human slavery. We've watched television docudramas on the subject. We're theoretically aware that it once went on, but chances are good that most of us have never witnessed it for ourselves.

Tragically, another category of slavery goes on every day in the lives of Christians.

But before we go there, let's grasp a mental picture of slavery. Back in the nineteenth century our sixteenth president realized something radical must be done about slavery in our country. Unwilling to look the other way any longer, on September 22, 1862, he presented what came to be known as the Emancipation Proclamation, an official document condemning human slavery.

Abraham Lincoln, realizing that slavery is completely against human dignity, officially abolished it from the United States on that day. Tragically, little changed in the daily life of our nation, even though the slaves were officially declared free. You know why; you've read the stories. The Civil War was still going on. The plantation owners never informed their slaves. The vast majority of the former slaves couldn't read, so they had no idea what the news was carrying. There was no mass media then to announce those kinds of presidential pronouncements.

And so for the longest time, slavery continued even though it had been officially brought to an end.

The war ended in April 1865. Do you know when Lincoln's declaration was officially enacted? When the people finally began to leave their enslaved lives and make their way toward freedom? December 18, 1865—more than three years after he first released his proclamation. Lincoln had been dead for months.

The word traveled out of the streets of Washington and down into the Shenandoah Valley of Virginia, across the back roads of the Carolinas and into Georgia, then Alabama, then Mississippi, then Louisiana, then Texas, then Arkansas, announcing what had been true for more than a thousand days. Even then the word somehow either wasn't believed or wasn't acted upon. Those officially emancipated people, thinking slavery was the way they were condemned to exist, continued to live in bondage though they had been declared free men and women since the fall of 1862.

Now if you think that seems shocking, let me tell you something equally as shocking: believers in Jesus Christ still live enslaved to the domination of a power that no longer has power over them. What has freed us is the great Emancipator, Jesus Christ, whose death on the cross set us free from the law of sin and the fear of death. Like an Emancipation Proclamation, it was made known to the world at large: Satan is defeated! Sin is overwhelmed! Death no longer has its sting!

Listen to our Emancipation Proclamation, our Freedom Statement: "Our old self was crucified with Him, in order that our body of sin might be done away with, so that we would no longer be slaves to sin" (Rom. 6:6).

In simple terms, this freedom liberated us from the necessity to sin. Truth be told, you don't *have* to sin. You know why you sin? Because you *want* to! That doesn't sound very affirming but it's the ugly truth. Every time you sinned last week, you wanted to. The same this week. You weren't forced to. It certainly wasn't the new nature operating within you. You gave in to the old nature that you had been enslaved to so much of your life. As a Christian living like this, you are under the false impression that you are as you've always been and things are just the same as they've always been: "There's just that part of me that I can't help. I just react like that. It's just the way I am."

But it's not the way you have to be. It's the way you choose to be.

Think of it like this. You're driving in the mountains. You come to a very sharp series of curves. The state officials who work with traffic signs have options. They can build a clinic at the bottom of the curve so that when you go over the cliff and crash, emergency vehicles can come quickly to help you. Or they can put up a sign that says, "SLOW, CURVE AHEAD."

The favorite verse 1 John 1:9 is the clinic at the bottom of the hill. It's mercy after the fact. The Lord *is* faithful to forgive us our sins. After we've sinned, thank God we are able to go to Him and say, "Lord, today I blew it" or "I reacted in a way that wasn't appropriate" or "I lusted," "I lost my temper," "Greed took over and I walked through it at the time knowing completely that I was doing what's wrong but I went ahead anyway. That's sin and I lay it before You, I confess that to You." That's the clinic.

But there's a better way! You can read the sign and react differently. You don't have to speed around this curve; you don't have to go over the cliff. You can slow down. When you realize that you're faced with a temptation, you can stand up against it. You don't have to yield to it. That's what Romans 6 means when it says we should no longer be slaves to sin: "He who has died [in Christ] is freed from sin" (v. 7). It doesn't mean we're freed from ever sinning again; it means we're freed from its domination.

I can live my life in such dependence on the Spirit of God that the flesh does not get its way for an extended period of time. Now I can never live free of it because the old nature hasn't been eradicated. But thanks to the power of God I can be on the side of such victory in my life that I walk a whole new kind of life.

SET FREE FROM THE OLD ME

When Christ came to live in our lives at the time of our conversion, the Spirit of God took up residence. We've already discussed the fact that the Spirit of God is now living within us. We have His power. That's the power of the triune God living in us. When He takes up residence, we are set free from our former master's domination. The Holy Spirit comes to give us a completely new kind of life . . . a life lived on another plane. Lived above guilt and shame, lived above the fears of life. He enables us to live as victors and not victims.

The old nature is still there but you don't have to listen to it and you don't have to spend time with it. You certainly don't have to yield to it or live under its control. You can live *above* that level if you really understand and accept the benefits of the grace of God. That's what Romans 6:11 is all about: "Consider yourselves to be dead to sin, but alive to God in Christ Jesus."

See the word *consider*? The original term means "to calculate, to take into account." The habits that once defeated me, discouraged me, and deprived me of authority in life—all of those habits are gone. They no longer have control over me. As we saw before, verse 12 is the command: "Therefore do not let sin reign"—don't let it take control of your mind, your body, your life. Don't obey its promptings anymore. You were there long enough but you don't have to live there anymore. The slave shack in which you once lived has been burned to the ground, leaving you able to walk away and never return. Please listen to me—*you're free!*

NOT MY MASTER ANYMORE

Not long ago, I had a terrific thing happen at the Dallas-Fort Worth airport. DFW is one of the reentrance portals through which our troops return home from fighting in Iraq. Folks often gather to applaud them and raise high their "Welcome home" signs and streamers. The evening newscasters swarm the troops with lights and cameras. People applaud. Families embrace. Smiling children wave American flags. It's a wonderful scene.

A number of people from our church and other churches were there to thank these men and women, some of them still bearing the physical and emotional scars of war as they got off the plane. With all our attention directed at the returning troops, it was easy to overlook a body of raw recruits standing nearby who were about to go to the Marine Corps Recruit Depot. They were just about to start their lives as young Marines. I guess the drill instructor had brought them to the airport to observe one of the few times in the Corps that they would be applauded. He wanted them to see what they had to look forward to.

Let me tell you, that drill instructor was taking these guys to task! He was barking orders right and left. It was great to stand in the background and watch the scene unfold. I reflected on my former Marine days, more than fifty years ago. I recalled the endless harassment. This drill instructor was doing the same thing.

He walked close by where I was standing and I said, "How you doing there, Sarge?"

He said, "Fine, sir, thank you."

It was the first time a drill instructor ever said "sir" to me in my whole life. What a great moment!

Why would he do that? Because I'm not his recruit. I'm not under his domination. He no longer has authority over me. Back in 1957 I lived at his mercy . . . I obeyed every word, but no longer. I can speak to him like I can anybody else.

That's exactly what I must do with my old nature.

Listen: you have spent long enough living under the dominating thought that you're a helpless victim of your urges and sinful drives, living as if you can't say no. When, in fact, living within you is a power that exists for the purpose of giving you a whole new way of life and introducing you to a different way of life. It's a grace-oriented lifestyle.

If I have one wish for the body of Christ it is that we would live in light of the victory we have in Christ and let the joy of grace characterize our lives rather than the frowning demands of the law.

The old nature is done getting its way. Our new nature, the one that the Spirit controls, is smoothing our path. That happens when we stop presenting our drives, our urges, our thoughts—that which is in the innermost parts of our beings—to sin as instruments of unrighteousness. You and I are not subservient slaves anymore. Instead, we present ourselves to God as those alive from the dead and our members as instruments of righteousness to God. In other words, we deliberately and intentionally put Romans 6 into action.

We can live our lives in such a wonderful way that sin takes a backseat. That's when grace really unfolds and we live in the liberty the Spirit provides, with all the blessings of freedom that go with it. Romans 6:14 declares, "Sin shall not be master over you, for you are not under law but under grace." See the options? To be under law is to accept the obligation to keep it and to live under its curse, its condemnation, its demands, and its irksome requirements. We're not there any longer. The law has done its best work when it has brought us in submission to Christ. But the other side is "under grace."

I like the way the J. B. Phillips paraphrase renders the same verse: "Like men [and women] rescued from certain death, put yourselves in God's hands as weapons of good for his own purposes. For sin is not meant to be your master."

And *The Message* reads this way:

> You must not give sin a vote in the way you conduct your lives. Don't give it the time of day. Don't even run little errands that are connected with that old way of life. Throw yourselves wholeheartedly and full-time—remember, you've been raised from the dead!—into God's way of doing things. Sin can't tell you how to live. After all, you're not living under that old tyranny any longer. You're living in the freedom of God. (vv. 12–14)

Are you hearing this? Then stop the habit of obeying your former drill instructor! He's no longer in charge of you.

Now, if you don't know Christ, all of this is simply tantalizing information. It sounds too good to be true. But it's truth that you're missing by not knowing Christ.

Tragically, you're surrounded by Christians who live as though they don't have Christ.

You and I need to train ourselves to change our thinking. It's time to move from the shack we've lived in far too long into the brand-new world Christ has designed for us to live in by the power of His Spirit.

THE PROBLEM OF SIN

Why am I camping on this so long? Because old habits are hard to break. We're addicts curbing our own sin. We don't have the ability to do that. We must now abide in One who does that for us. We must learn to rest in Him, rely on Him, give our everyday lives over to Him.

May I personalize this? You can't stop lusting on your own. You can't stop greed on your own. You can't stop your own temper. But the One who lives within you has the ability to put the brakes on all that and so much more.

"Who will set me free from the body of this death?" (Rom. 7:24). No one other than the Holy Spirit. In Him we find a brand-new power that enables us to do the things we can never do within ourselves.

If it were not for the all-conquering power of the Spirit of God, the whole Bible would end with those five words, also from verse 24: "Wretched man that I am!" But there is so much more! It's magnificent to know that our God has come to our rescue and has marvelously provided a power we don't have in ourselves.

God's Provision for Today

Have you started to feel hopeless in the midst of your wretchedness? The good news is the Spirit of God is available to you. Right now! I love the word "now" in Romans 8:1: "Therefore there is *now* no condemnation for those who are in Christ Jesus" (emphasis mine). God's provision for the believer is not on hold until we're in heaven, it is right *now*. When the Spirit of God takes over, He breaks us loose and frees us from the work of the flesh so that we're able to enjoy the depth and beauty of that free-flowing river that never will run dry.

When we live a Spirit-filled life, the Spirit produces a different mind-set in us. "Those who are according to the flesh set their minds on the things of the flesh, but those who are according to the Spirit, the things of the Spirit" (Rom. 8:5). What a difference that new mind-set makes! The Holy Spirit doing His work in us creates within us a hunger for righteousness, an interest in spiritual truth, an authentic spiritual mindset.

That mind-set, described in verse 6, offers a vitality of life and inner peace: "The mind set on the flesh is death, but the mind set on the Spirit is life and peace."

There's a vitality of life. There is an inner peace that comes from the Spirit. Along with His transforming presence, His divine life is in us (vv. 9–10).

It's called *justification*. We have been declared righteous. (How great is that?) Don't go to bed tonight laboring over all the stuff of your life that you've blown. He forgives you. He sees you as righteous. Because of justification, we are considered godly ones.

The old nature is still there; we still have the option of living according to the flesh, which is the fallen, egocentric human nature and a sin-dominated self that drives us mad. Again, think of it this way: the third member of the Trinity is living within us!

How to Live Free

As I think of this ongoing struggle between the old man and the new man in Christ, I thank God for His relief. How grateful I am for the cool breezes that the Spirit brings on my hot and barren soul. The Spirit sets me free. As you go into another day of walking with Christ, lift your face to the sky, feel the refreshing breeze. Think repeatedly, "I am free!"

Remind yourself of three truths:

First, only God can bring relief to a soul this wretched.

Only God can come to your rescue when you have

made such a mess of things. You cannot handle it by yourself. Your flesh desires expression and it's constantly producing sinfulness. Even though you have come to the cross, even though the Savior lives in your heart, in your life, in your soul and spirit, there is still this old nature that craves to be satisfied. When the Holy Spirit is in control He helps you find that satisfaction in God.

Second, learn to recognize that a life lived in the energy of the flesh centers on self.

You will discover that you can detect a sinful mindset at work by how much life revolves around you—your comfort, your desire, your plans, your importance, your pedigree, your degrees, your accomplishments. Paul said, "I came to the place in my life where all of that was like raw sewage. I had no ground to stand on when I realized God wanted to be first in my life." A life lived in the energy of the flesh centers on self—on "It's all about me." That attitude keeps us proud and leaves us miserable. It's the word "wretched" all over again.

Third, a life lived with the Spirit in control leads us into grace.

Grace keeps us humble and sets us free. Let's do a quick fly-over of Romans 8 and see all the grace that is ours in Christ:

- *Life and peace*: "For the mind set on the flesh is

death, but the mind set on the Spirit is life and peace" (Rom. 8:6).

- *Absence of fear and an intimacy with God*: "For you have not received a spirit of slavery leading to fear again, but you have received a spirit of adoption as sons by which we cry out, 'Abba! Father!'" (Rom. 8:15).

- *Inner assurance . . . doubts gone*: "In the same way the Spirit also helps our weakness; for we do not know how to pray as we should, but the Spirit Himself intercedes for us with groanings too deep for words; and He who searches the hearts knows what the mind of the Spirit is, because He intercedes for the saints according to the will of God" (Rom. 8:26–27).

- *Inner awareness that "all things" are working together for good and God's glory*: "And we know that God causes all things to work together for good to those who love God, to those who are called according to His purpose" (Rom. 8:28).

I close this chapter by underscoring the value of authentic humility in the believer's life. Humility is essential if we hope to receive grace and the Spirit's help. Just as you have a heavenly Father, just as you have a magnificent Savior, you have the power of the very presence of God living and at work within you. You may *feel* trapped by sin . . . but the truth trumps that feeling: "The law of the Spirit of life in Christ has set you free from the law of sin and of death" (Rom. 8:2).

The Spirit does for us what we cannot do for ourselves. It is a magnificent switch, a transforming change that gives you the strength you don't have in yourself. He does through us what we cannot pull off, even with the best intentions or the most sincere of New Year's resolutions. We cannot do it on our own, but the Spirit of God fulfills it *in* us and *through* us.

Let Him. I plead with you, let Him take over. When you do you will discover firsthand what it means to be embraced by the Spirit.

∽ 6 ∽

CAN I BE PROMPTED BY THE SPIRIT TODAY?

There are times we don't know how to describe what's going on inside us. When we are at a loss to know the solution to some particular problem, we wrestle and wonder through a great deal of uneasiness. We struggle over how we're going to get through it or how we're going to make a decision. On the one hand, it looks good this way—but on the other hand, it seems wrong. Then, something happens that changes everything. Something occurs in the unseen realm of our spirit that changes us. We now feel this is right to pursue. Or we are assured this is wrong and we don't. Amazingly, we look back on those times and feel so grateful that, at the time of decision, the right choice was made.

There are other occasions when we can't understand what the Scripture is teaching. We're dealing with a verse or a passage and we can't grasp what it's about. So we pray and we wait. We also check other verses and fall back on what we have been taught. In addition, we go to books or talk to people we respect. But still, nothing seems to break through. Then, out of the blue, the light clicks on and we get it. We *see* it. Everything finally becomes clear.

In the first situation, I would say *intuition* came through. We just felt like we should or shouldn't do something. The second situation describes *insight*. We got an insight into some truth that we had been wrestling with over a period of time. I have experienced both of these, as I'm sure you have too.

I'd like to explore a third phenomenon different from intuition or insight. Let's call these experiences "unidentified inner promptings"—UIPs for short. (Not to be confused with UFOs.) UIPs are those hunches, those uneasy moments that say, "Don't go there" or "Watch out—danger!" or "There's a lot of risk here." Or "This is right . . . it's where you ought to go."

This is outside our five senses; we're now dealing with a subjective field that is difficult to address. Nevertheless, since we're thinking about the workings of the Holy Spirit, we need to address the reality of UIPs. Unless I miss my guess, you have experienced them. Perhaps right now you are on the verge of a decision and you don't know what you ought to do. You've prayed, you've checked the Scriptures, you've sought counsel. At some point in God's time you'll have a breakthrough and you'll know what you ought to do. How does that happen? Why does that happen? Let's explore this fascinating realm of the Spirit's working.

CREATED FOR CONNECTION WITH GOD

In the early account of creation we get a clue into how God communicates with us. The climax of the creative week is, of course, the creation of humanity. God brings Adam and Eve on the scene—created "in God's image" (Gen. 1:26–27). This makes them altogether distinct. The plants were not made in God's image; neither were the animals. The stellar spaces did not bear His likeness—only the man and the woman did.

God communicates with His own people in a way that He does not communicate with animals. Animals have instinct; we have image. We have an inner, "secret chamber" within our being; the Scriptures call it our "heart." It's where the Lord speaks to us. He directs us with inner promptings. He urges, He moves, He convicts, He stops, He guards, He guides. That explains why Solomon wrote, "Watch over your heart with all diligence, for from it flow the springs of life" (Prov. 4:23). We'd say, "Guard that spirit of yours." When God made us, He gave us a body *and* an immaterial soul and spirit.

Anyone who studies the creation account has to pause

here and let some of the wonder in. We need to ask and answer: What is this "image of God"?

Whatever it was, originally, by the time we get to Genesis 5, that image has changed. If you remember, between Genesis 1 and Genesis 5 sin invaded and polluted the human race. Adam and Eve were no longer innocent; they were now sinners and distant from God. They were even hiding from Him! When their family came along, the difference in the image of their boys was noteworthy. Genesis 5:3 says, "When Adam had lived one hundred and thirty years, he became the father of a son *in his own likeness*" (emphasis mine).

See the difference? The original creation of man and woman is in God's likeness, but when Adam and Eve had a son, he was in Adam and Eve's likeness. Something significant had changed about that image.

One theologian wrote, "Sin damaged the created ideal, but that damage must not have been complete. For this reason, one may say that the image of God has been defaced but not erased. It has been tarnished but not destroyed." What are we saying? Only this: Adam was originally created to have that sense of connection and communication with the One who made him. That broke down when sin entered the scene. That communication wasn't erased; it was effaced. It wasn't destroyed; it was damaged. The same is true with us today. We live with a defaced and damaged image. Nevertheless, unlike animals, we are able to connect with our God in the inner person like our pets never can and never will.

INSIGHT FROM THE PSALMS

Psalm 139 is fast becoming my favorite psalm. As David wrote it, he was focusing on the magnificent hand of God in his life.

Verse 1: "You have searched me and known me." Is there any greater intimacy?

Verse 2: "You know when I sit down and when I rise up; You understand my thought from afar." In other words, "Long before I have the thought, You already know it's there. You understand it."

Verse 3: "You scrutinize my path and my lying down, and are intimately acquainted with all my ways." When our kids were young, we bought them an ant farm. We spent hours together watching the ants as they busily moved around inside their clear plastic world, as they normally do underground. We studied the way they made intricate paths in the dirt.

That's the thought that comes to my mind here.

The Lord sees us just that clearly—in fact, more clearly. He not only sees our paths, He knows our motives. He knows our words before we say them. He knows our thoughts before we think them. So it is with our Creator.

Verses 13–14: "You formed my inward parts; You wove me in my mother's womb. I will give thanks to You, for I am fearfully and wonderfully made; wonderful are Your works, and my soul knows it very well." Watch how the probe of God's Spirit drives us to the very life of the embryo, the fetus, in the womb of the expectant mother. As we realize how God put us together, there is a tangible wonder, a fearful realization that we're different, distinct from creation.

Now I'm going to risk making a statement I know will polarize opinions. Reading this, you may be skeptical or you may very well be relieved that someone finally agrees with you. Here we go: I believe there are times the only way God can communicate with us, whether it is through conviction or assurance or direction or reassurance or encouragement, is through unidentified inner promptings (UIPs). Let's stop calling them "coincidences" and "hunches" and "feelings." We need to identify them as the work of the Spirit.

IN THE CAVE WITH A VICTORIOUS, DEFEATED PROPHET

The Hebrew prophet Elijah had a UIP after one of the greatest events of his life. If you recall in 1 Kings 18, Elijah stood toe to toe against King Ahab and his wicked wife, Jezebel. Ahab dared to stand against the living God, so Elijah called for a showdown on Mount Carmel between the God of Israel and all of Ahab's 450 prophets. It was one of history's greatest standoffs.

As you would expect, the pagan priests were wrong, Elijah was right, and all the prophets of Baal were wiped off the scene. This incensed Jezebel. She delivered a dramatic threat to Elijah: "So may the gods do to me and even more, if I do not make your life as the life of one of them by tomorrow about this time" (1 Kgs. 19:2). Only the Bible could say it like that! We would say, "Elijah, you're finished. Tomorrow at this time you'll be in the past tense."

In a moment of weakness, perhaps exhausted from the standoff at Carmel, perhaps weary from the drought that had swept across the land, and altogether worn out from fighting against false prophets and demonic forces, Elijah caved in and ran for his life. He traveled as far as he could from Jezebel. He ended up in the Judean wilderness, alone in a cave, asking God to take his life.

Ever been there? It would probably surprise you today to know how many people you know that would say yes. Elijah was thinking wildly and, for sure, unbiblically. "I have no reason to go on! It's *all* over." He was in a cave. Ultimately the Lord asked him, "What are you doing here, Elijah?" (1 Kgs. 19:9).

Good question, Elijah. In His tender mercy toward the depressed prophet, God was particularly kind to give him a dramatic display of communication. God told Elijah to go stand on the mountain.

> And behold, the LORD was passing by! And a great and strong wind was rending the mountains and breaking in pieces the rocks before the LORD; but the LORD was not in the wind. And after the wind an earthquake, but the LORD was not in the earthquake. After the earthquake a fire, but the LORD was not in the fire; and after the fire a sound of a gentle blowing. (1 Kgs. 19:11–12)

If you're reading from the King James Version of the Bible that last phrase is rendered, "a still small voice." But "voice" is not mentioned in the original Hebrew text. Instead it should be translated "a gentle rustling."

You know what I call it? An unidentified inner prompting. God got through to Elijah's spirit, and He touched him as nothing in the sensory world would have grasped. Earthquake, wind, fire—none of that moved him, but there, in that gentle rustling, God revealed Himself to Elijah. The result is that Elijah wrapped his blanket around him and walked *toward* God rather than *away* from Him. It's a tender moment. God provided relief for this beat-up and weary prophet in the form of rest, sustenance, and a partner in ministry until Elijah was taken off the earth years later.

If there's anything that troubles me about our culture and our times, it is the noise and the pace of it all. Those things work against the voice of God quietly speaking to reach us. I warn you about being so busy you miss His voice. Back off. Take time to listen. God's voice may be in the earthquake or the fire. There are messages there. But often, His inner promptings will come in the deep well of our spirit, for He simply says, "Yes, go there" or "Wait" or "No. Stay away from that." Slow down. Cool your jets. Take time to listen.

TROUBLE AHEAD!

In the latter seasons of the apostle Paul's life, he knew he was headed for trouble. On one occasion, he said, "And now, behold, bound in spirit, I am on my way to Jerusalem, not knowing what will happen to me there, *except that the Holy Spirit solemnly testifies to me* in every city, saying that bonds and afflictions await me" (Acts 20:22–23, emphasis mine).

I find that a very significant declaration. It was, in fact, a UIP! "I've been with the Lord, seeking His guidance, and He told me, 'You're to go to Jerusalem, Paul.' But there's also been that inner sense, that spoken rustling of the Spirit communicating, 'But beware, there's trouble ahead.'" Sure enough, there was. Paul was arrested more than once and sent to Rome where ultimately he was imprisoned, had an audience before Nero, and was finally beheaded. But all the troubles started in Jerusalem, just as the Spirit told him it would happen.

But look at Paul's bold response. "But I do not consider my life of any account as dear to myself" (Acts 20:24). In other words, "I'm not troubled knowing there are trials ahead. My goal is to 'finish my course and the ministry which I received from the Lord Jesus, to testify solemnly of the gospel of the grace of God'" (v. 24).

Haven't you ever wondered how persecuted believers, not only in the first century but in the twenty-first century, could endure suffering? How do they endure it? Now we know. The Spirit of God not only gives them an awareness of danger but also the confidence that they can bear up under it. That explains how some of the Reformers could be burned at the stake and, while being burned, offer up their prayer to God that God would forgive those who were taking their lives.

That courage and presence of mind comes from this inner prompting of the Spirit saying, "It is going to be dreadful for you, but I will give you the strength to endure." The glorious reality is that God is not finished giving His people that kind of strength in hard times. I have experienced it, especially in the last three years of my life. On occasion, I didn't know how I could go on. Most people, except my wife and family, knew nothing of it. Throughout those times, I had to rely on the reassuring presence of the Spirit of God to stay at it.

Some of you are there right now. You know in advance that if you take the journey that's in front of you, there will be trials. But the "gentle rustling" of the Lord says, "I am with you. I will give you the strength." Such UIPs can be wonderfully reassuring.

UIPs in a Great Storm

If you love the sea and enjoy sailing, you owe it to yourself to read Acts 27. This is another example of the Spirit of God at work, even when danger is near. Paul was on a ship with over two hundred people as the quintessential perfect storm swept across the Mediterranean. The Holy

Spirit reassured Paul that they would be going down, but no one's life would be lost.

Paul spoke to his fellow companions and the seasoned sailors, "Men, I perceive [UIP in progress] that the voyage will certainly be with damage and great loss" (v. 10). Ultimately there was a shipwreck but they all were rescued because the sailors heeded Paul's warning. All got wet, but all were safe.

The good news in times of potential or present danger is that the Spirit of God can provide peace. In fact, Paul had such peace that he sat down and had a meal with the sailors before the shipwreck. (Picture that!) He encouraged them to "keep up your courage, for there will be no loss of life among you, but only of the ship" (v. 22).

How did he know it? Another example of Spirit-given inner promptings.

PROMPTINGS IN PRAYER

One more from the life of Paul.

Paul led a pretty extraordinary life once God got ahold of him on the Damascus Road. As a result, he could have gotten awfully proud and puffed up. But the Lord in mercy didn't allow that to happen. He gave Paul a thorn in the flesh. There are all kinds of surmising about what this "thorn" was, but this we know for sure: it was physical, it was painful, and it was designed to keep him humble. Paul described it, "Concerning this I implored the Lord three times that it might leave me" (2 Cor. 12:8).

Sounds familiar? You've prayed about a situation but nothing happens. So you pray again and still nothing happens. And you pray with greater intensity and nothing happens. We've all been there. In this case, God answered Paul with, "No. I'm not going to take away the thorn. You're going to live with that." Somewhere in the processing of that difficult news, Paul received a UIP, an unidentified inner prompting that said, "[God] has said to me, 'My grace is sufficient for you, for power is perfected in weakness'" (v. 9).

Paul's response? "Most gladly, therefore, I will rather boast about my weaknesses, so that the power of Christ may dwell in me. Therefore I am well content with weaknesses" (vv. 9–10). (What a great attitude!)

In our years of walking with the Lord, most of us have learned that He blesses times of our great weakness with great favor. If you have ever carried out His will and His work in a weak manner, you may also have seen Him empower you and bless it.

The Lord has used sermons that I have preached in times when I struggled with something so severely that

I could hardly push my words out of my throat. Later I found out that those sermons ministered to people in ways unlike any other I've preached. I can't explain it other than the mercy of God rests on us in our weakness.

Dr. Richard Halverson left his long-term pastorate at Fourth Presbyterian Church in Bethesda, Maryland, to become the chaplain of the Senate. He suddenly felt inadequate. In his words, "I felt like a non-person among the Congress. I felt like a mascot to one of the most powerful political bodies in the world. I wondered what I was doing there."

That evening, he read the words of Jesus: "All authority has been given to Me in heaven and on earth. . . . And lo, I am with you always" (Matt. 28:18, 20). Halverson said, "As I meditated on those words, I realized, I am a garment which Jesus Christ wears every day to do what He wants to do in the United States Senate. I don't need power; my weakness is an asset. If Christ is in me, what more do I need?"[1]

If you feel like you don't have great gifts or you haven't been used in a great way, here is hope for all of us. Have you known weakness? Scripture is true when it says there is a great contentment with weakness knowing that "when I am weak, then I am strong" (2 Cor. 12:10).

How can you be confident of that? The inner prompting of the Spirit says, "It's okay that you're weak.

It's okay if you're losing your voice and you're the soloist for the day. It's okay if you don't feel like you're as well prepared as you should be. It's okay. In your weakness, God will make up the slack."

I do want to wave a flag of caution here in specific circumstances:

- When you're not sure the UIP is from the Spirit . . . back off.

- If you sense this is contradicting the written Word of God . . . get away from it.

- If you sense this may not be coming from the Spirit . . . don't mess with it.

- If you think there might be some demonic influence in it . . . firmly resist, or flee.

Those are all promptings that you shouldn't pursue. However, the flip side of that is when you are confident it is from the Lord . . . go for it!

Let me add one last thing: be ready for a surprise. Correction, be ready for a *lot* of surprises!

If in any way you feel like your season of fruitfulness has come to an end, be encouraged by Charles McCoy's true story. Charles was a Baptist preacher, pastoring a church in Oyster Bay, New York. At age seventy-two, he was mandated by his denomination to retire. A lifelong bachelor, he had cared for his mother for as long as she lived. In his spare time, he had earned seven university degrees, including two PhDs—one from Dartmouth, the other from Columbia. Being forced to retire from the ministry, he fell into a deep depression.

> I just lay on my bed thinking that my life is over. I haven't really done anything yet. I've been a pastor of this church for so many years, and nobody really wants me that much—what have I done for Christ? I've spent an awful lot of time working for degrees, but what does that count for? I haven't won very many to the Lord.

A week later he met a Christian pastor from India, and on impulse (UIP), Dr. McCoy asked him to preach at his church. After the service, the Indian brother asked him matter-of-factly to return the favor (UIP). Since he had preached for McCoy, would McCoy come to India and preach for him? McCoy told him he was being asked to retire and move to an assisted-living home down in Florida, but the Indian pastor insisted, informing McCoy that where he came from, people respected a man with white hair. Would he come?

McCoy thought and prayed about it and finally decided (UIP!) he would. The members of his church were aghast. Dire predictions were made. The young chairman of the board of deacons summed up the attitude of the congregation when he asked, "What if you die in India?"

I love McCoy's answer. He told him he reckoned "it's as close to heaven from there as it is from here." He sold most of his belongings, put what was left in a big trunk, and booked a one-way passage to India—his first trip ever out of the United States.

When he arrived in Bombay, he discovered to his horror that his trunk had been lost, never to be found. All he had were the clothes on his back, his wallet, his passport, and the address of missionaries in Bombay he had clipped from a missionary magazine when he left. He asked for directions, got on a street car, headed for their house. When he got there, he discovered that while on the street car, his wallet and passport had been stolen.

He went to the missionaries, who welcomed him in, but told them that the man who had invited him to come to India was still in the United States and would probably remain there indefinitely.

What in the world was he going to do now? Unperturbed, McCoy told them he had come to preach and that he felt (UIP!) that he would try to make an appointment with the mayor of Bombay. They warned him that the mayor was very busy with ultra-important matters. In all the years they'd been missionaries there, they had never succeeded in getting an audience with him—not even once. Nevertheless, McCoy set out for the mayor's office.

The next day, he was invited in. When the mayor saw McCoy's business card listing all the degrees, he reasoned McCoy must be not only a Christian pastor, but someone much more important than that. Not only did he get an appointment, the mayor held a tea in his honor attended by all of the big officials in Bombay. Dear old Dr. McCoy was able to preach to those leaders for half an hour. Among them was a director of India's West Point, The National Defense Academy at Poona. He was so impressed at what he heard from McCoy that he invited him to the academy to preach to the students.

Thus was launched, at age seventy-two, a brand-new, sixteen-year ministry for Dr. Charles McCoy. Until he died at age eighty-eight, this dauntless man circled the globe preaching the gospel. There's a church in Calcutta today because of his preaching and a thriving band of Christians in Hong Kong because of his faithful ministry. What's interesting is he only ever had enough money to get him to the next place he needed to go. He died one afternoon in a hotel in Calcutta, resting for a meeting he was to preach at that evening. He had indeed found himself as close to heaven there as he would have been at his church in Oyster Bay or some retirement home in Florida.[2]

I *love* that story. Not because I'm planning to retire, but because God has a way of working and moving if we'll only listen to and obey His promptings, which sometimes come in that still, gentle rustling, and sometimes on the deck of a ship at sea, and sometimes when the people around you are saying, "There's no way you ought to go there," and sometimes in your feelings of great weakness and inadequacy. In spite of all these odds, He plans to use you in an incredible way. That's the story of our lives, isn't it?

Are you aware today that the inner prompting at work in your life is the voice of God? It is God's way of saying, "Pay attention, I'm speaking to you." Quit hiding behind the fact that you're weak, or that others are saying it's impossible, or that you feel like you're in danger, or that it's not a fire or an earthquake or a wind storm but a gentle rustling. Quiet your heart so that you can hear what He's saying. Stop closing doors that He is opening or trying to push open doors that He has closed. Ask the Lord to confirm when His unidentified inner promptings are reliable and are His Spirit's work. Allow the Spirit to draw you into His safe embrace and tell you something He intends for you to hear.

Be still and learn again that He is God. Be still.

DOES THE SPIRIT HEAL TODAY?

Ours is a world of enormous pain and hurt.

Every one of us knows someone who is enduring an intensely difficult time of physical or emotional trauma—or both. *Is it you?*

We know sincere people of faith who have prayed for healing in their lives . . . and still they suffer. They cry out to God but the heavens feel like brass. Nothing but silence—and the pain and hurt continue.

Then, to add salt to their wounds, they hear about someone who claims to have been healed instantaneously. They hear remarkable stories of miracles—someone attended a meeting where an individual with special "powers" touched them or simply spoke to them and *whoosh!* . . . the Spirit healed them of their affliction.

Why are some healed, while many—in fact, most—are not? Why can some look back and claim a miracle while others must endure excruciating years of exhausting pain?

Some would simply shrug this off as "some have faith, others don't." We're not going to do that. We believe in the living God just as much as those who claim they've been healed. We certainly respect His Son and uphold the work of the Spirit with equal sincerity and with passion. Yet we wonder how some could be relieved of an affliction almost overnight, while most must live with pain through lingering years of their lives. I know people right now in our church, even people in my own family, who wait for God to touch their lives and bring them back to a place of health they once knew. I also know others who were so sick they were rapping on death's door, yet only days or weeks later experienced healing and relief. All of this creates a dilemma within us. Needing to find answers to things that don't make sense, we are driven to do a serious study of this through Scripture.

"Have you heard of the Four Spiritual Laws?"

That question, found in a small booklet, has been asked and answered thousands—perhaps millions—of times in our generation. These "laws" have been used by God to introduce His plan of love and forgiveness to countless numbers of people who had no idea how to have a meaningful relationship with Him.

I have a similar question. It is designed to introduce some foundational facts to those who are confused over the painful circumstance they are enduring . . . and how the whole issue of healing applies to them.

HAVE YOU HEARD OF THE FIVE SUFFERING LAWS?

That question appears in no booklet—but it should! These "laws" will do more to help those who hurt and erase doubt and confusion than perhaps anything else you could read. All five are well supported in Scripture. They build on each other, so stay with me.

Law One: There are two classifications of sin.

1. *Original Sin*: the inherited sin nature traceable to Adam, original "head" of the human race. Ever since man's fall in Genesis 3, it has been impossible to be born into this world without sin. We get this sinfulness from our parents, who got it from theirs, who got it from theirs . . . all the way back to everyone's original parents, Adam and Eve. When Adam sinned, his act of disobedience polluted the stream of humanity, not unlike raw sewage pollutes a river. Romans 5:12 says, "Therefore, just as through one man sin entered into the world, and death through sin, and so death spread to all men, because all sinned."

Adam and Eve disobeyed, and the consequences were tragic. Suffering, sickness, and death were introduced into the human race, all stemming from sin. Had there never been sin, there would never have been suffering or sickness or death. Read again the inspired edict: "and so death spread to all . . . because all sinned." That's original sin.

2. *Personal Sin*: individual acts of wrong we regularly commit. Because we all have inherited a sin nature (the root), we commit sins (the fruit). Because all humans have this Adamic nature within, we commit personal sins. Instead of obeying, we disobey. Instead of choosing to walk with God, we resist Him, we run from Him, we even fight against Him. "For all have sinned and fall short of the glory of God" (Rom. 3:23).

We are sinners by birth (original sin), and therefore we become sinners by choice (personal sin). In acting disobediently, we bear the fruit of our Adamic root. Because deceit and disobedience rest in our nature, we rebel. Because lawlessness is at our inner core, we act it out in life. You act it out differently than I do, but we're both sinners—by nature and by practice.

Now, here's how this relates to illness . . .

Law Two: Original sin introduced suffering, illness, and death to the human race (Rom. 5:12b).

Had there never been the presence of original sin in the Garden of Eden, mankind would never have known sickness or death. In the broadest sense of the word, all sickness and suffering today is the result of original sin.

Literally, the Lord told Adam "in the day that you eat from it *you will surely die*" (Gen. 2:17, emphasis mine).

No one is immune from sin and its consequences. As beautiful and lovely as your little girl, boy, or grandchild may be, that child was born with a sin nature. And that nature not only prompts disobedience, it is the source of sickness, suffering, and ultimately death. Those things are a part of the "fallout" of the Adamic nature. Think of them as being interwoven in the tapestry of humanity.

Law Three: Sometimes there is a direct relationship between personal sins and sickness.

David testified of such in Psalm 32:3–5 and 38:3–5. Paul warned that some of the Corinthian believers were "weak and sick" and a number of them were dead (1 Cor. 11:27–30) because they were sinning.

At times, disobedience and rebellious acts are directly linked to some illness in the body.

Among the most notorious examples in Scripture would be King David after his affair with Bathsheba. As a result of his sinful behavior, David suffered grave physical and emotional consequences. The struggle he went through while hiding his adultery (including the murder of Bathsheba's husband) and living as a rebellious hypocrite led to such a crescendo of inner turmoil David became physically ill. After Nathan confronted David

and the king came to terms with his sin, he wrote a song
of remembrance . . . his own painful testimony of those
months of misery:

> When I kept silent about my sin,
>> my body wasted away
> Through my groaning all day long.
>> For day and night Your hand was heavy upon me;
> My vitality was drained away
>> as with the fever heat of summer. (Ps. 32:3–4)

David suffered intensely because he disobeyed God,
but he refused to face his sin. Guilt ate away at him
until it became so unbearable that he literally groaned
as he physically wasted away. He lost his appetite. He
suffered from insomnia. He could not think clearly or
lead decisively. He lost his energy. He suffered from a
fever that wouldn't go away.

Imagine that kind of life. If you have ever been there,
you don't need me to describe it. While they may not
have reached these proportions, most of us have known
painful periods in our lives when we left our personal sins
unaddressed and unconfessed. Our misery didn't leave
until we faced our sin and dealt with our disobedience.
That is what happened to David:

> I acknowledged my sin to You,
> And my iniquity I did not hide;

I said, "I will confess my transgressions to the LORD";
And You forgave the guilt of my sin. (Ps. 32:5)

What was it that made him sick? Guilt. What drained
his energy? Guilt. What took away his happiness, his smile,
his ability to think, his leadership skills? Guilt. There was
a direct relationship between David's personal sins and
the physical and emotional sickness that impacted his life.

Another example would be a discipline issue Paul
delivered in one of his letters to the Corinthians when he
corrects their inappropriate behavior at the Lord's Table.
Some, if you can believe it, used this as an occasion for
gluttony and drunkenness. The apostle's words of reproof
are powerful: "For this reason many among you are weak
and sick, and a number sleep" (1 Cor. 11:30).

In other words, their sin had resulted in weakness and
sickness . . . and even in death!

Now remember, in such cases, the confession of sin
begins the process of healing. The recovery is usually not
instantaneous, though on occasion it is. More often than
not, however, the suffering begins to fade in intensity as
the person experiences relief from guilt.

*Law Four: Sometimes there is no relationship between per-
sonal sins and sickness.*

Some are born with afflictions—suffering before they ever
reach the age of committing sins (John 9:1–3; Acts 3:1–2).

Others, like Job, are living upright lives when suffering occurs (Job 1:1–5). Jesus Himself does "sympathize with our weaknesses" (Heb. 4:15) rather than rebuke us because we have sinned. Remember, "Although He was a Son, He learned obedience from the things which He suffered" (Heb. 5:8). Jesus never committed sins, yet He suffered.

This is a good time for me to extend a compassionate caution. You are not called to be God's messenger to every person who is ill, telling them, "There must be something wrong in your life." Occasionally you may be the appointed Nathan in some David's life. You may be the chosen one to say, "You are the man" or "You are the woman." But seldom do we have a right to say that. In many cases suffering or illness is not the result of personal sin.

A classic example of this would be the man in John's gospel who was born blind. His congenital blindness had nothing to do with personal sins, either his own or his parents'. In John 9:1–3 we read that when Jesus and His disciples were walking through the streets, they saw a man blind from birth. His disciples asked, "Who sinned, this man or his parents, that he would be born blind?" Jesus answered, "It was neither that this man sinned, nor his parents; but it was so that the works of God might be displayed in him."

Jesus stated clearly that the man's physical affliction had nothing to do with personal sins.

Hebrews 4:14–15 also comes to mind: "Therefore, since we have a great high priest who has passed through the heavens, Jesus the Son of God, let us hold fast our confession. For we do not have a high priest who cannot sympathize with our weaknesses, but One who has been tempted in all things as we are, yet without sin."

If our weaknesses were always the result of sin, the writer would say, "Confess your sins and you will be healed." But he said here, in effect, "Seeing us struggling with weaknesses, our Lord is moved over our affliction. He is touched with our struggles." He didn't say, "Deal with the sin in your life and you will recover." On the contrary, His heart is moved over your pain. He grieves with you over the length of your depression. He sits alongside you in the hospital room as you live with the consequences of a dreaded malignancy . . . He is with you as you go through chemotherapy. He is touched with feelings of sympathy for you in your weaknesses.

Why? Because on those occasions, there is no direct relationship between personal sins and sicknesses.

I have known people who have been gravely ill and have searched their heart to find the sin that caused their affliction. They confess and plead and beg for forgiveness. But their illness doesn't leave. Slowly, painfully, they waste away, wondering what they could have done that caused their sickness . . . when, in fact, their condition was not at all related to personal sin.

Law Five: It is not God's will that everyone be healed.

Those who believe it *is* invariably support their convictions with the words of Isaiah 53:5b: "By His scourging we are healed." "There is healing in Christ's atonement!" they shout. Of course there is! But the context is talking about Christ's priceless provision for man's inner, spiritual needs. By His scourging we are *spiritually* healed. That is why He was wounded and bruised. That is why He died . . . not to heal sick people but to give life to dead ones.

Take Paul. As we learned earlier, he asked God to remove a "thorn in the flesh." The Greek term translated "thorn" means a sharp stake. Whatever that thorn was, it brought piercing pain. When the pain reached the unbearable stage, this devoted servant of God begged God to take it away. Three times he made the same request: *Heal me.* Each time God's answer remained firm: *No* (2 Cor. 12:7–9).

Following that traumatic struggle he stated he was "well content with weaknesses" because *without healing* the Lord proved Himself sufficient and strong (2 Cor. 12:10).

Paul calls this "thorn" a messenger of Satan (obviously allowed by God) to keep him genuinely humble.

Pain does that. You don't meet many arrogant people who are living with lingering pain. Pain buffets us; it breaks and humbles us.

Sometimes it is not God's will that we be healed. Be very careful not to promise healing to a person who is sick. If it were God's will for all people to be well, then there would be no sick people in the world. Or if it were the Lord's will to heal all those in His family, not one Christian would be ill.

Learn to think biblically. Think theologically. God is with us in our pain. His Spirit often ministers healing in ways other than just physical. Simply because He chooses not to bring healing does not mean He is not at work. He is with you through the hardest time. His grace is still sufficient.

The corollary to Law Five: Sometimes it is God's will that someone is healed.

There are times when our Lord sovereignly chooses to "restore the one who is sick" (James 5:15). This is His sovereign prerogative. When He miraculously intervenes, the healing is immediate, thorough, permanent, and free. When that happens, He alone deserves the praise—never some human instrument. It's all in God's hands. Don't look for healings around every corner. God is not in the sideshow business. If miracles were commonplace, they would become "regulars."

Every time healing happens, God has done it. It occurs daily. Occasionally it is miraculous. More often, it is aided by proper diagnosis, expert medical care, essential medicinal assistance, and good old common sense. When God heals there is no way man can grab the glory.

Most Christians I know would not hesitate to say that the Lord heals. We have seen Him bring healing to fractured marriages, broken lives, and scarred emotions. Who of us would doubt then that He could heal physical and mental diseases? Why else do we pray for Him to intervene when we or someone we love gets sick? He who creates life can certainly bring healing to it.

I have a wonderful mental list of individuals whom I have known, prayed for, and stood with through times of great and threatening sicknesses. Today they are strong specimens of health. In many cases the attending physicians virtually gave up on them. I am convinced— and I assure you *they* are convinced—the Lord healed them.

However, the most disillusioned believers I have ever spent time with have been those who were promised healing by alleged healers and it wasn't to be. That is borderline tragedy to witness. My heart goes out with great compassion to whoever suffers—whether it be my twelve-year-old grandson or some eighty- or ninety-year-old saint afflicted or paralyzed or a victim of some disease.

There they are. The Five Suffering Laws regarding sin, sickness, health, and healing.

Law 1: There are two classifications of sin.
Law 2: Original sin introduced suffering, illness, and death to the human race.
Law 3: Sometimes there is a direct relationship between personal sins and sickness.
Law 4: Sometimes there is no relationship between personal sins and sickness.
Law 5: It is not God's will that everyone be healed.
And its corollary: Sometimes it *is* God's will that someone is healed.

Read each one again. Write them in the back of your Bible. Sure as the world you are going to run into someone who will wonder why he or she (or a loved one) is not being healed. Maybe God will use your words to calm that person's anxiety and remove his or her confusion.

What Do You Do with Your Pain?

Though I am not normally a worrier, I am more than slightly concerned over what people do with their pain, their brokenness, and especially their need for relief. There are so many unbiblical and erroneous answers being offered that will only deceive, disillusion, and disturb you. They will, in fact, bring greater confusion.

"Expect a miracle" can be devastating when the miracle doesn't occur. People are told that something is wrong with them, that they are harboring sin, that they are not strong enough in their faith, and on and on. Sufferers are being promised miracles by many alleged authorities—some are sincere, some naïve, some professional con artists—and when the miracle does not come, the damage done is always tragic and occasionally irreparable.

And so it's with that in mind I turn your attention to some sound theology without apology. Sound theology is the basis of experience; experience is not the basis of theology. Teaching the Word of God is my responsibility, not telling people what they want to hear. Assuaging their guilt or relieving their pressure or salving their wounds does them no good. But we can be sure that God's truth sets us free.

Earlier, we flew by a verse in James that we now need to return to for a closer look, along with its surrounding verses.

"Is anyone among you sick?" James asked in his letter. The term translated "sick" is the Greek word *astheneo*, which means "to be weak, to be without strength." It suggests even "to be disabled, to be incapacitated." This is a serious illness.

Now let's walk, step by step, through the Spirit's instruction to James about what to do when someone is suffering.

"Is anyone among you sick? Then he [the sick one] must call for the elders of the church" (5:14a). First, the sick person takes the initiative. Often the elders and other church leaders are the last ones to know when someone is sick. Sometimes those who are ill feel neglected and even think that pastors and elders really don't care when, in fact, they don't even know. Step one is clear: let them know.

Second, when the elders arrive, they carry out two functions. "They are to pray over him, *anointing him with oil* in the name of the Lord" (v. 14b, emphasis mine). The anointing with oil *precedes* the time spent in prayer.

There are two Greek words for *anoint*. One always has a religious and ceremonial connotation; the other a practical one. David's head was anointed with oil before he came to the throne of Israel. It was a ceremonial anointing, acknowledging that he was the king-elect. However, you would never tell someone that you "anointed" your bike with oil because the chain was squeaking or that you "anointed" the hinge on the door with oil. Such a procedure is practical. It has no religious connotation at all. Now, of the two words, it is the latter that is used here, the practical one. "Rubbing" would be a better rendering of that word rather than "anointing."

When the Good Samaritan took care of the man who had been beaten along the road to Jericho, he poured oil and wine into the man's wounds. He "rubbed" those ingredients into the man's wounds. The same term appears in ancient Greek medical treatises where oil was prescribed for the purpose of medication.

Anoint in James 5 refers to the practical application of proper medicine, or, in today's terms, to the appropriate professional help as well as prescribed medications. In other words, "See your doctor and follow his instructions." That comes first. Then, after seeking appropriate medical attention, there is to be prayer.

I strongly believe in following this process. I find it very hard to pray for someone who refuses to consult a doctor and follow his or her orders, or who refuses to take the prescribed medication or follow the recommended therapy. I believe it is biblical for those who are seriously ill not simply to seek medical attention, but to do that *first*.

I have admired for decades Dr. C. Everett Koop, the former United States surgeon general. Over the span of his career, Koop performed over fifty thousand operations. In the book *The Agony of Deceit*, Dr. Koop wrote a chapter

entitled "Faith-Healing and the Sovereignty of God."
You'll find this insightful:

> A surprising number of Christians are convinced
> God will not be believed unless He makes tumors
> disappear, causes asthma to go away, and pops eyes
> into empty sockets. But the gospel is accepted by
> God-given faith, not by the guarantee that you will
> never be sick, or, if you are, that you will be miracu-
> lously healed. God is the Lord of healing, of grow-
> ing, of weather, of transportation, and of every other
> process. Yet people don't expect vegetables without
> plowing. They don't expect levitation instead of get-
> ting in a car and turning a key—even for extraordi-
> narily good and exceptional reasons.
>
> Although God *could* do all of this, Christian
> airline pilots do not fly straight into a thunderstorm
> after asking God for a safe corridor, although He
> could give them such safety. While we pray for a
> speedy discovery of successful treatment, I must do
> all I can to employ medical science in its task, as all
> health care professionals must do.[1]

Not enough praise is given to those who serve the sick
in the field of medicine—physicians, nurses, therapists,
etc. What a fine and necessary body of caring people.

But they are not miracle workers. They do not pretend to be. But they have received careful training and therefore have wisdom and understanding needed by those who are sick. Many of them who are Christians have a quiet, sincere appreciation for the Spirit of God in the midst of their profession. If our Lord cared enough about medication to mention it in a passage such as this, it certainly should be honored and applied in our age of advanced technology.

Sometimes healing is instantaneous. More often than not, though, recovery from illness takes time—under the care and watchful eyes of a competent physician. It is important to remember that the Holy Spirit is involved in both kinds of healings, not just the miraculous ones. It is easy to overlook during the long and often anguishing months (sometimes years) of recovery.

In the process of finding relief from sickness, medical assistance and proper medication play an important role. Remember, however, following the oil, they were to pray. As men of faith, genuinely committed to God's will being carried out, the elders would have prayed fervently, believing, offering up strong, confident, and yet humble prayers of intercession.

Third on the list we find in James 5: specific results are left in the Lord's hands. "In the name of the Lord" (v. 14). God's will was sought, not the empty promises of some earthly individual. Doing something "in the name of the Lord" was a colloquialism in that day for "the will of God." Today we might say, "Have them apply the oil, then pray for God's will to be done."

The result? "And the prayer offered in faith will restore the one who is sick" (v. 15).

Be careful to keep verses 14 and 15 together in context. The elders are to pray over this person in the name of the Lord—that is, asking for God's will and His blessing—and the result? It's in God's hands. When it is His sovereign will to bring healing, it will occur. In that case, "the prayer offered in faith will restore the one."

There is another important term here: "and the Lord will raise him up" (v. 15). This looks miraculous to me—a case of instantaneous healing. And don't overlook the additional comment: "If he has committed sins, they will be forgiven him" (v. 15).

Perhaps the person's past was marked by sins—extended, serious sins. If this is the root of the problem, there will be an admission of it in the process of the healing. (Remember our Third Law: there is often a direct relationship between personal sins and physical sickness.)

Let's not miss verse 16: "Therefore, confess your sins to one another, and pray for one another so that you may be healed. The effective prayer of a righteous man can accomplish much."

"Confess your sins to one another" is not a general public acknowledgment before the whole church of every dirty, wayward, lustful thought you have had. The verse refers to a person who is ill and who knows that he or she is living a lifestyle that is wrong and therefore needs to bring that out into the open, to confess it to those who are spiritually concerned and praying for him or her. The result? Cleansing within . . . healing without.

As we carefully work our way through these instructive verses in James 5, several timeless principles emerge, all of which are worthy to claim today.

Confession of sin is healthy—do it.

When you find that you are wrong, say it. When you have done something offensive to another person, go to that individual and openly admit it. Confess it to God and then find the person you have hurt and confess it to that person. God honors such unguarded vulnerability. Full confession can lead to full restoration.

Praying for one another is essential—practice it.

When someone says, "Will you pray for me?" take the request to heart. Don't glibly respond, "Oh, yeah, sure," then promptly forget about it. Ask for some details. Write down the specific requests. I have a little notepad on my desk in my study, and when someone requests prayer, I write down the person's name and needs. I won't remember if I don't write it down. Later on, I often follow up and ask if God has answered prayer.

Medical assistance is imperative—obey it.

Regardless of the ailment, the nature of the illness, or the excuses you may be tempted to use to cut that corner, seeking medical assistance is both wise and helpful. And whatever the physician prescribes or suggests—obey!

When healing comes from God—claim it.

Praise Him for it. Don't give credit for your healing to some person on this earth. God alone is responsible for your relief. Healing doesn't come because you pay someone for it or stand in line for it or appear before some individual who claims he or she is able to do it. Healing comes because God sovereignly and mysteriously chooses to say yes to you. It falls under the heading of undeserved favor—*grace*.

God is able to do what He pleases with whomever He chooses whenever He wishes. His Spirit, alive in us, is all-powerful. But He is also sovereign; He has the right to choose whom He will, for whatever purpose He would be delighted in, for His glory, at whatever time He may select.

WHEN HEALING TAKES TIME

One final thought on how the Spirit's embrace brings healing to our lives. I'm thinking now of the one who is called to endure suffering—those who have sought healing and to whom the Lord has said yes, but it'll take some time.

Let me speak directly to you who hurt. God is doing some of His best work in you in the time it takes to heal. Almost imperceptibly, you are becoming a person with keener sensitivity, a broader base of understanding, and a longer fuse! Patience is a by-product of lingering pain. So is tolerance with others and obedience before God. It is difficult to know how to classify these characteristics, but for lack of a better title, let's call the whole package *Spirit-given wisdom*.

For too many years in your life you may have operated strictly on the basis of knowledge—the human absorption of facts and natural reaction to others. But affliction has now entered your life, and even though you would much prefer to have it over with, it has not ended. The pain you are forced to endure is reshaping and remaking you deep within.

David the psalmist once wrote,

Before I was afflicted I went astray,
But now I keep Your word. . . .
It is good for me that I was afflicted,

That I may learn Your statutes. . . .
I know, O LORD, that Your judgments are righteous
And that in faithfulness You have afflicted me.
(Ps. 119:67, 71, 75)

David admitted that a much greater desire to obey (v. 67), a much more teachable spirit (v. 71), and a much less arrogant attitude (v. 75) were now his to claim, thanks to prolonged affliction.

Human knowledge comes naturally. But with it there often comes carnal pride; a sense of self-sufficiency; and tough, arrogant independence. This kind of knowledge can cause us to become increasingly less interested in spiritual things. As our reservoir of horizontal knowledge grows, our skin gets thicker and often our hearts become harder.

Then comes pain. Some physical ailment levels us to mere mortality. Or an emotional collapse. A domestic conflict explodes, and we are reduced to a cut above zero. Whatever it may be, we're paralyzed, we feel cast adrift in a sea of private turmoil and possibly public embarrassment. To make matters worse, we are convinced we will never recover.

At just such a dead-end street, divine wisdom waits to be embraced, bringing with it a beautiful blend of insight—the kind we never had with all our knowledge—

genuine humility, a perception of others, and an incredible sensitivity toward God. During the time it is taking us to heal, wisdom is replacing knowledge. The vertical dimension is coming into clearer focus.

HIPPOCRATES' "HEALING IS A MATTER OF TIME"

Hippocrates was a Greek physician considered by many to be "the Father of Medicine." It was he who wrote the Hippocratic Oath taken by those entering the practice of medicine. He lived about 450 to 375 BC, which made him a contemporary of such philosophers as Socrates, Plato, and Aristotle. Hippocrates wrote much more than the famous oath that bears his name, and most of his writings, as we might expect, have to do with human anatomy, medicine, and healing.

In a piece entitled *Aphorisms*, for example, he wrote: "Extreme remedies are very appropriate for extreme diseases." In *Precepts*, these words appear in the first chapter: "Healing is a matter of time." While reading these recently, it occurred to me that one might connect them in a paraphrase that would have a rather significant and relevant ring to it: "Recovering from extreme difficulties usually requires an extreme amount of time."

In our world of "instant" everything, that may not sound very encouraging. Yet, more often than not, it is true. The deeper the wound, the more extensive the damage, the greater amount of time is needed for recovery. Wise counsel, Hippocrates!

Where would the old Greek get such wisdom? His *Aphorisms* and *Precepts* sound almost like the Proverbs of Solomon.

Hippocrates lived sometime between Solomon the king and Paul the apostle—what is known in biblical history as the between-the-Testaments era, that four-hundred-year span when no Scripture was being written, although the Old Testament books were being compiled. Could it be that the Greek physician-philosopher, in his research, came across some of Solomon's writings and rephrased a line or two? For example, isn't it possible that something from Solomon's journal (Ecclesiastes, by name) could have found its way into Hippocrates' writings? Consider the first few lines:

> There is an appointed time for everything.
> And there is a time for every event under heaven—
> A time to give birth and a time to die;
> A time to plant and a time to uproot what is planted.
> A time to kill and a time to heal;
> A time to tear down and a time to build up.
> (Eccl. 3:1-3)

Tucked away in that third verse is the intriguing phrase,

"a time to heal." I cannot help but wonder if Hippocrates' words, "Healing is a matter of time," might have found their origin in Solomon's statement. In any event, the statement remains sound, both medically and biblically. Except in cases of God's miraculous intervention, healing takes time. And the greater the disease or damage, often the longer it takes to heal.

I have been concerned about this issue for a long time. Throughout my years in ministry I have met so many people who hurt, with the pain coming from every conceivable source.

Those who have seemed most disillusioned, however, have been the ones who prayed for but did not experience a quick recovery. Many of them were promised such by people who held out the hope of a miracle. When the anticipated divine intervention did not transpire, their anguish reached the breaking point. I have looked into their faces and heard their cries. I have witnessed their response—everything from quiet disappointment to bitter, cursing cynicism . . . from tearful sadness to violent acts of suicide. And most have been sincere, intelligent, Christian people.

A FINAL WORD FOR THOSE WHO HURT

God allows our suffering. Don't doubt for a moment that circumstances of suffering are used by God to shape you and conform you into the "image of His Son." Nothing enters your life accidentally—remember that. There is no such thing as "luck" or "coincidence" or "fate" to the child of God. Behind our every experience is our loving, sovereign Lord. He is continually working things out according to His infinite plan and purpose. And that includes our suffering.

When God wants to do an impossible task, He takes an impossible individual . . . and crushes him. Being crushed means being reshaped—to be a vital, compassionate, useful instrument in His hands.

The apostle Paul puts his finger on a critical insight to learn during any season of suffering: that we might come to a complete end of ourselves and learn the power of total dependence.

When Paul's own strength had ebbed away, he found another strength. When his own will to go on faded like that last morning star, the sun of a new hope blazed on his horizon.

When he finally hit bottom, Paul learned that he was in the palm of God's hand. He could sink no lower than the Everlasting Arms.

Perhaps I am writing to a stubborn, suffering saint who is wrestling with God over an affliction. You have not yet laid down your arms, rested your case, and decided to trust in Him completely.

Can't you see, my friend, that God is trying to teach

you the all-important lesson of submission to Him—total dependence on His infinite wisdom and unbounded love? Trust me here: He will not let up until you give up. Who knows that case-hardened independence within you better than God? How much longer are you going to fight Him? In Psalm 46:10, He urges us to cease striving—be still.

The Lord is near . . . more real than the pain you are enduring. His Spirit longs to support you in the crucible of your crisis. Trust Him today. His Spirit stands ready to embrace you if you will only invite Him to do so. Right now.

He will hear you.

He has a special love for those who hurt.

How Can I Experience the Power of the Spirit?

We've come full circle. When we began our journey on the Holy Spirit, we were with the Lord Jesus and His disciples in the Upper Room. It was the night Jesus was arrested, followed by the day He went to the cross. During that Last Supper, Jesus prepared His men for life on earth after His departure. He promised them that He would not abandon them in that desperate place; "I will not leave you as orphans; I will come to you" (John 14:18). Jesus also promised them that His replacement would be "another Helper," namely, the Holy Spirit (v. 16). In addition, when that other Helper came, He would become an integral part of their lives. He would not only be with them temporarily; the Spirit would reside within them for the rest of their years on earth. Jesus had only been *with* them; He (the Spirit) would be *in* them.

The last words Jesus' disciples heard from His lips as He returned to heaven were an extension of that promise:

"You will receive power when the Holy Spirit has come upon you" (Acts 1:8). His Spirit would not only help them—but He promised His disciples *power* when the Spirit came to reside in them.

To those men in that era, that heaven-sent, undeniable power from the One whom Jesus dispatched manifested itself in dozens of different ways, many of them visible and supernatural. They were empowered to stand and preach before the public, unashamed and unafraid. They experienced such dynamic internal changes that they were given the ability to speak in languages and dialects previously unknown to them. Many of them performed miraculous feats, while others healed diseases instantly and permanently. They discerned error, confronted evil, raised the dead, and endured the most torturous of deaths without flinching. Amazing transformation!

Something revolutionized those timid, awkward, fearful disciples, turning them into bold, devoted, inspiring men of God . . . and that something was a supernatural source of power.

To be sure, that transitional interlude was a unique era as the infant church was born and began to grow. It was a period of time when miracles authenticated God's presence in human lives and God's message through human lips. Without the completed Scriptures, how would people know who were the anointed of God?

Furthermore, in spreading the gospel rapidly across vast unevangelized regions, the ability to speak in many languages and dialects was invaluable. Clearly, it took enormous power to launch the *ecclesia*, the church.

BUT WHAT ABOUT THE POWER OF THE SPIRIT TODAY?

What are the evidences of Spirit-filled power today? Can we—should we—expect "a miracle a day"? Should "supernatural power" be the watchword of every believer? Is something wrong with us if we don't consistently manifest the Spirit of God's phenomenal presence and mighty workings?

The disciples had earlier heard Jesus talk about the Spirit. In John 7 Jesus described Himself as living water and then laid out a glorious invitation: "If anyone is thirsty, let him come to Me and drink" (v. 37). He also promised something for us: "He who believes in Me [that includes you and me!], as the Scripture said, 'From his innermost being will flow rivers of living waters.' . . . This He spoke of the Spirit" (vv. 38–39).

Let me paraphrase verse 38: "From the believer's inner life there will be a reservoir of enormous, immeasurable power. It will gush forth. It will pour out like a torrential river, creating rapids and waterfalls and strong currents to the oceans." That's the idea. It's not a picture of some blasé, passive kind of latent force that hopefully will be there. It is the dynamic of life, called simply "the Spirit."

The most powerful force in your life as a Christian is something you can't even see. It is so powerful it holds you eternally till Christ comes and secures your destiny, ushering you right into eternity. In the meantime He is ready to work within you, transforming your life. The Spirit's power is waiting to be used.

God's Word does not toss around the word *power* loosely; nor are we personally promised supernatural manifestations on a day-to-day basis. However, the Spirit's power in control of the life of a believer is nothing short of phenomenal. Let's return to basics to be reminded of this altogether magnificent power.

UNDERSTANDING FIRST THINGS FIRST

How would you complete these two sentences?

I am a Christian because_____ .
I am filled with the Spirit when_____ .

What does it mean to be a Christian? How can a person say with assurance that he or she is a member of God's forever family? Let's allow God's Word to answer that for us: "But as many as received Him, to them He gave the right to become children of God, even to those who believe in His name" (John 1:12).

Is it that narrow? Is becoming a Christian limited solely to knowing Christ? Again, let's let Jesus answer that for us. John 14:6 says, "Jesus said to him, 'I am the way, and the truth, and the life; no one comes to the Father but through Me.'"

No question about it, that is an exclusive statement. But the truth is as narrow as Christ has declared it, and it is truth because He said it. The first sentence I asked you to complete could read as follows: I am a Christian because *I am rightly related to the Son of God.* First Timothy 2:5 confirms, "For there is one God, and one mediator also between God and men, the man Christ Jesus." In this pluralistic culture, it is worth noting the singular: "one God . . . one mediator."

What must I do then to get the source of God's power into my life? This may surprise you, but the answer is *nothing.* He comes to live within you instantly and permanently when you are rightly related to the Son of God . . . when you believe in Christ. You don't make a single contribution to your standing before God by doing this or promising that or giving up certain things. The transaction is based on grace—God's matchless, unmerited favor. When you and I receive the gift of eternal life, wrapped inside that gift is the Holy Spirit.

He comes as part of the "initial salvation package." We are never commanded to pray for the Holy Spirit or to be baptized by the Holy Spirit or to be regenerated by the Holy Spirit or to be sealed by the Holy Spirit. Why? Because all of those things occur at the moment we are born anew.

Let's suppose you have in your hands a book I gave you as a gift. What if you were to say to me, "I would really love to have every chapter of this book." I would say, "You have all the chapters. They are all there and they are all yours to read and enjoy. You have the book; therefore you have everything in it." So it is with Christ. Upon receiving Him, we have everything that comes with the gift of salvation . . . and that certainly includes the presence and the power of the Holy Spirit.

This brings us to the second sentence:

I am filled with the Spirit when *I am rightly related to the Spirit of God.* When we are, the power within us is unleashed and we become His vessels of honor, ready and available for whatever service He wishes us to perform. When we are filled (living under the Spirit's control), the power that raised Christ from the dead becomes the motivating force within our lives. Think of it!

As we learned earlier, the filling of the Spirit not only means that our lives are totally available to God, but it also includes such things as keeping short accounts, being

sensitive to whatever may have come between us and Him
. . . and walking in complete dependence upon Him.

When we do, He is able to work through us, speak
through us, use us, direct us without restraint, and
empower our gifts; we need His power, His working,
His cleansing, His freeing. And as He fills us, all that
and so much more take place.

How Do I Know Christ Is at Work?

So, then, you may ask, "What is realistic to expect of the
Christian life. How can I see this power at work? How
do I know that Christ is at work?" Numerous things
come to mind.

*Because I am a Christian and therefore rightly related to
the Son of God:*

- I am in Christ.
- I live in Him and He lives in me.
- I know the relief of being cleansed from personal
  sins.
- I am able to live above sin's dominating control.
- I have immediate access to the Father through
  prayer.

- I am able to understand the Scriptures.

- I am able to forgive—and should forgive—whoever wrongs me.

- I have the capacity to bear fruit daily, continually, routinely.

- I possess at least one (sometimes more than one) spiritual gift.

- I worship with joy and with purpose.

- I find the church vital, not routine or boring.

- I have a faith to share with others.

- I love and need other people.

- I look forward to having close fellowship with fellow Christians.

- I am able to obey the teaching of the Word of God.

- I continue to learn and grow toward maturity.

- I can endure suffering and hardship without losing heart.

- I depend on and trust in my Lord for daily strength and provisions.

- I can know God's will.

- I live in anticipation of Christ's return.

- I have the assurance of heaven when I die.

Don't rush through that list. Each bullet point is quite amazing. This sampling illustrates all kinds of unique possessions, experiences, and blessings that are yours by God's grace to enjoy simply because you have been accepted into His family. They are yours to claim every day. When you add them all together, you'll certainly agree that they represent an impressive list of incredible realities.

While none of the above would be considered *miraculous*—at least in the usual sense of the term—they certainly fall into the category of *remarkable*. When we remind ourselves that these are normal and that they are continually ours to enjoy, the Christian life becomes the most enviable lifestyle imaginable.

This may not be "power Christianity," but it is certainly the "abundant life" Christ promised. Make sure to get that straight or you will live your life disappointed and frustrated, always looking for something more ecstatic or over-the-top supernatural.

Several years ago a seasoned pilot told me that flying an airplane consists of hours and hours of sheer boredom, interrupted periodically with split seconds of sheer panic.

While I would never use the word *boredom* to describe the Christian life, you get the point. God can (and sometimes does) step into our world in supernatural ways and manifest His power. It is remarkable how He interrupts the routine (if we could call the things I listed routine) with something phenomenal that only He could have done.

Let me suggest another list for you to ponder. These are things you and I can claim when the Spirit is in full control.

When you are Spirit-filled and therefore rightly related to the Spirit of God:

- You are constantly surrounded by the Spirit's omnipotent shield of protection.

- You have an inner dynamic with which to handle life's pressures.

- You are able to be joyful . . . regardless.

- You have the capacity to grasp the deep things of God that He mentions in His Book.

- You have little difficulty maintaining a positive attitude of unselfishness, servanthood, and humility.

- You have a keen sense of intuition and discernment; you sense evil.

- You are able to love and be loved in return.

- You can be vulnerable and open.

- You can rely on the Spirit to intercede when you don't even know how to pray.

- You have no reason to fear evil or demonic and satanic assaults.

- You are enabled to stand alone with confidence.

- You experience an inner assurance regarding decisions.

- You enjoy a clear, shame-free conscience.

- You have an "internal filtering system."

- You can actually live worry free.

- You are able to minister to others through your spiritual gift(s).

- You have an intimate, abiding "Abba relationship" with the living God.

Again, none of the things on the list above could be called *miraculous.* They are neither super-phenomenal in nature nor supernatural manifestations, but they are yours to claim simply because the powerful Spirit of God is filling you. This is not "power filling," but the normal, wonderful, Spirit-filled life.

Frankly, these evidences are the things we need and can count on far more than exceptional moments of sheer ecstasy. These are the things we can count on because we are rightly related to the Son of God and to the Spirit of God. We do not need continual, highly charged "power visions" or "power encounters" nearly as much as we need to be filled with the sustaining, all-powerful Spirit of God. When He takes charge His power becomes evident.

Every child of God who walks in the power of the Holy Spirit is "freed up" to enjoy incredible release from the things that would otherwise hold us in bondage. What great liberty! "Now the Lord is the Spirit, and where the Spirit of the Lord is, there is liberty" (2 Cor. 3:17).

Liberty is another word for *freedom*. Freedom from what? Freedom from constraint and from fear. Freedom from tedious perfectionism. Freedom from a confining, boring, predictable life. Freedom from relational bondage. Freedom from addictions. Freedom to be, to do, to become. Such freedom comes from simply having the Spirit and allowing Him to fill us. It is a quiet, gentle release from all that binds us so that we can be whole, completely authentic. Inner reluctance departs. When in grief, we are free to cry. When experiencing joy, we are free to laugh. Authenticity flows freely and easily.

PRACTICAL EVIDENCES OF GOD'S SPIRIT AT WORK

The Spirit of God works deeply and intimately to transform our lives. He passionately desires to direct our steps, cleanse our thoughts, heal our wounds, take over our worries, reveal God's will, and protect us from evil. All this and so much more are ours through the dynamic presence of the One whom Jesus sent to be our Helper.

Don't let it trouble you that you cannot see or hear the Spirit at work. He operates in an invisible realm. This is a power and a force you will never see with earthly eyes; you will only see its working. The metaphor Scripture uses is that the Spirit is like wind. You can't see it but you see its work (John 3:8).

When He, the Spirit of God, is in control, it is awesome. When He is absent, it is dreadful.

Let's think about this in practical terms. Just how do you see the Spirit at work?

We see the Spirit at work in our personal lives.

We can know the Spirit's presence by witnessing it in our own lives. You know who you were before you came to Christ. You know how your attitudes and motivations have changed. The Spirit's work is continually going on. Paul stated very clearly that our bodies represent the Spirit's temple: "Or do you not know that your body is a temple of the Holy Spirit who is in you, whom you have from God, and that you are not your own? For you have been bought with a price: therefore glorify God in your body" (1 Cor. 6:19–20).

When you are a child of God, the Spirit Himself bears witness with your spirit that you are a child of God

(Rom. 8:16–17). When we are with other Christians, the witness of the Spirit verifies our spiritual connection, even though we may speak different languages and come from differing cultures. It's a wonderful connection. I can sit down with a body of believers in Russia and feel an immediate sense of accord, a real family identification, even though I don't speak a word of Russian. That is the Spirit's working.

Furthermore, when we encounter enemy attacks, the Spirit's work is obvious when we have a sense of confidence and security in our faith. We know that "greater is He who is in you than he who is in the world" (1 John 4:4).

We see the Spirit empowering gifted Christians for ministry.

Those gifts and ministries differ and vary, but the same Holy Spirit is at work. First Corinthians 12 lays out a fabulous catalog of gifts, "but the same Spirit" (v. 4). A variety of ministries, "and the same Lord" (v. 5). A variety of effects, "but the same God who works all things in all persons. But to each one is given the manifestation of the Spirit for the common good" (vv. 6–7).

When I hear a gifted teacher expound the Scriptures, I am benefiting from the Spirit's work in that person's life. When I hear of or see people who are gifted in evangelism winning people to Christ, I know the work of the Spirit is involved. When I see people actively showing mercy and encouragement, demonstrating hospitality, and helping others, I am again witnessing the work of the Spirit.

We see the Spirit convicting sin.

> He, when He comes, will convict the world concerning sin and righteousness and judgment. (John 16:8)

You may not believe it but those without Christ struggle with their unbelief. It's a fact. They try every way in the world to escape it—through a bottle, through drugs, through travel, through activity, through education or some kind of philosophical meanderings, through advanced education, through good causes, through hobbies or some other means of escape. They try to run from the Spirit who is drawing them to salvation. Yet the Spirit convicts the world of sin and of righteousness. He is like an ever-present prosecuting attorney saying, "These are the facts. Here is the evidence. There is the guilty." And they are shut up without excuse in light of facts and evidence. How does He do this? Through the believers in Christ whom He indwells.

The child of God living on this earth, empowered by the Spirit of God, is a living letter observed by the world. As the world observes you and me controlled by the Spirit, the world witnesses a transformed life. And as that incredible life is carried out in a unique way in the same world where others are failing or frustrated, they become aware that there is a radical difference. And the Spirit of God convicts them of their unbelief in Jesus Christ as they discover your source of power. When the Spirit of God comes, He will convict the world of sin. They will be aware of sin, not by looking at the mountains that tell of the glory of God, the nature that reveals the majesty and power of God, but by witnessing living truth in your life and in mine.

If nothing else, this truth will motivate a godly life when you realize you are, in fact, the *only* Bible that many read who come in contact with you. You're writing the Gospel of John, chapter 16, tomorrow morning at work. You're finishing it tomorrow afternoon, and you're writing the seventeenth the following morning. You're writing a gospel and the world reads it. They will discover it is either truth or falsehood, depending on how closely your life squares with Scripture. The Spirit of God uses your life to reach lives.

The second part of John 16:13 is for the believer. We see the Spirit guiding us into truth.

During my tour of duty in the Marines, our troopship sailed into Yokohama harbor in January of 1958. Though years had passed since the end of World War II, that harbor was still a place of danger because of underwater mines that had not yet been removed. At the mouth of the harbor, our ship stopped and took aboard a Japanese harbor pilot to lead us through the treacherous waters. Slowly and cautiously he steered us through those dark, uncharted waters. As we stood on deck, we could see nothing but the surface below us and the harbor ahead of us. But the harbor pilot steered the ship with confidence, knowing every turn to take to bring us safely to the pier.

In the same way, Jesus promised that the Helper would guide us into all the truth, steering us through life, pointing out the hidden rocks and the reefs and the mines ahead. While we see only the surface, He sees into the depths and far beyond the horizon.

We see the Spirit restraining lawlessness.

> For the mystery of lawlessness is already at work; only *he who now restrains* will do so until he is taken out of the way. (2 Thess. 2:7, emphasis mine)

Have you read the news on the Internet or watched the evening news lately? Granted, the world does seem chaotic and out of control. Lawlessness appears to be at an all-time high. But what would this world be like if the controlling influence of the Spirit of God suddenly disappeared? When the restrainer (the controlling power of the Spirit) is removed, there will be expressions and outbreaks of evil like we have never witnessed and cannot imagine. The Spirit is an envelope of righteousness, a bubble of purity. He holds evil in check. When He is removed, literally hell will break loose on this earth. We may think, *It can't get any worse* . . . but it will. When the restrainer is lifted from this earth, it will indeed! But for now we know His work is evident because He continues to restrain lawlessness.

We see the Spirit regenerating the lost.

> That which is born of the flesh is flesh, and that which is born of the Spirit is spirit. Do not be amazed that I said to you, "You must be born again." (John 3:6–7)

He is still expanding the ranks of the church. Not a week goes by that I don't witness or read or hear about the wonderful decision someone has made to follow Christ. That is the Spirit of God at work, leading people to Christ . . . still building His church. Yes, the Spirit is still at work transforming lives. He is still touching people. Still using folks like you and me. The Spirit of God is fully alive and well on Planet Earth. His ministry is far from over!

Never doubt that the Spirit of God is always at work. You can't see Him, just as you cannot see air, but you can feel Him. You know He is present. On some occasions it is almost as though you can touch Him. When He moves among a body of people, they are mobilized and empowered. They are motivated. They are cleansed. They are purged. They are en route to a proper destination. When He is absent, life is dreadfully, desperately empty. It's like a living death.

As we begin to wrap things up, let me ask you to imagine what it means to have the presence of the living God within you. Just think, the third member of the Godhead, the invisible yet powerful person of deity, living inside your being. You think you can't handle what life throws at you? You think you can't stand firm or stand alone in your life? You think you can't handle its temptations? Well, you can't . . . alone. But filled by His Spirit, with the very power of God put into operation, you can handle anything. The weight of pressure and anxiety will all be shifted from you to Him. It's wonderful.

Christianity rests on the power of the person of Jesus Christ. He brought us to salvation. He is the one who enables us to live the salvation lifestyle through His Spirit. When I yield myself to Christ, I trust His Spirit to take over. When I do, I am embraced by the Spirit.

It comes down to this: let God lead. It works against our nature because we are adults and we're strong, we've had training, we're educated, we're capable. Forget all that—let God lead. Release your grip, don't try to control the situation, and He will take you to places that will make your mouth drop open in wonder. Let God lead.

Some time ago I came across a little piece titled "The Road of Life."

At first, I saw God as my judge, keeping track of the things I did wrong, so as to know whether I merited heaven or hell when I die. He was out there sort of like a president. I recognized His picture when I saw it, but I really didn't know Him.

Later on when I met Christ, it seemed as though life was rather like a bike ride, but it was a tandem bike. I noticed that Christ was in the back helping me pedal.

I don't know just when it was that He suggested we change places, but life hasn't been quite the same since then. When I had control, I knew the way. It was rather boring, but predictable . . . It was the shortest distance between two points. But when He took the lead, He knew delightful long cuts, up mountains, through rocky places at break-neck speeds, it was all I could do to hang on! Even though it looked like madness, He'd lean back and say, "Pedal!"

I worried and was anxious, and asked, "Well, where are You taking me?" He laughed and never answered, and I started to learn to trust Him. I forgot my boring life and entered into the adventure. And when I'd say, "I'm scared," then He would lean back and He would touch my hand.

I didn't trust Him at first, not in control of my life. I thought He'd wreck it; but He knows bike secrets, He knows how to make it bend and take sharp corners, how to jump to clear high rocks, He knows how to shorten scary passages.

I'm learning to just shut up and pedal. We go to the strangest places together. I'm beginning to enjoy the view and the cool breeze on my face with my delightful companion, Jesus Christ.

And when I'm sure I just can't do any more, He smiles and says . . . "Pedal!"

I have lived long enough and gone far enough to be able to tell you something with complete confidence: to live a life embraced by His Spirit, with His Spirit fully in control, is not only an adventure, it's an amazing lifestyle. The heights and depth and insights are beyond your wildest imagination. You'll find yourself saying, "Thank You, Lord, for living Your life through me." Every day of my life I'm surprised. Better, I am awestruck by all that means.

In a short time, you'll be finished with this book.

Can I ask you to do one thing? Simply sit in silence for a few moments before the Lord. Looking back, you may see things that need attention. Or it may make you smile as you realize how gracious God has been. When you think ahead, you may feel twinges of fear. It's a great moment to tell Him that. Ask Him for reassurance and a sense of peace. Ask Him to fill your life with His Spirit, surrendering all that you say and do, all that you are, to His control.

I often begin my day by saying, "Lord, I don't know what the day holds but You do. I don't know what's in it for You or me, but I'm Yours. I invite You to guide me one step at a time. I want Your power to mark my steps. Stop me if I'm moving in the wrong direction. Push me if I'm sluggish. Get me going again if I'm hesitant. Correct my course if I get out of line. But don't let me go my own way. Fill me with Your presence and power."

The Spirit is not imaginary. He's real and relevant. He is able to turn each of our days into something beautiful, something useful for God's glory and for our good.

Let Him lead, my friend. You'll be surprised by His power. You'll be embraced by His Spirit. It's not simply a *great* way to live . . . it's the only way to live.

Notes

Introduction

1. Stuart Hample and Eric Marshall, *Children's Letters to God* (New York: Workman Publishing, 1991), 6–44.

Chapter 1

1. Archibald Thomas Robertson, *Word Pictures in the New Testament Volume III: The Acts of the Apostles* (Nashville: Broadman Press, 1930), 10.

2. F. F. Bruce, *Commentary on the Book of Acts* (Grand Rapids, MI: Eerdmans, 1954), 38–39.

Chapter 2

1. Robert E. Coleman, *The Master Plan of Evangelism* (Old Tappan, NJ: Revell, 1964), 23.

2. Ibid., 22–23.

3. Max DePree, *Leadership Jazz* (New York: Doubleday, 1992), 14–15.

Chapter 4

1. Henry Blackaby, *Experiencing God* (Nashville: Broadman & Holman Publishers, 1994), 196.

2. Henri Nouwen, *The Inner Voice of Love* (New York: Image Books, 1999), 34.

Chapter 6

1. Leighton Ford, *Transforming Leadership,* (Westmont, IL: InterVarsity Press, 1993), 15.

2. Franklin Graham, *Bob Pierce: This One Thing I Do* (Dallas, TX: W Publishing Group, 1983), n.p.

Chapter 7

1. C. Everett Koop, "Faith-Healing and the Sovereignty of God," in *The Agony of Deceit,* ed. Michael Horton (Chicago: Moody Press, 1990), 169.

Overview

Chuck Swindoll leads you in discovering more about the Holy Spirit's role in your life and how your deepening relationship could be the key to unlocking your desire to be closer to God. If you're ready to unlock some long-overdue passion and joy in your walk with Christ, find out how your relationship with God's Spirit is the answer.

Read

Introduction (pages 5–10); Jeremiah 29:13; John 10:10

Questions

1. Read page 5. Which do you identify with most—the first paragraph or the second? How does your answer describe what you hope to gain from reading about the Holy Spirit? Share with your group or with a friend one hope you have related to this new study.

2. In three words or less, describe what you think of when you hear, "Holy Spirit." What kinds of feelings do you attach to that description? Fear? Concern? Excitement? Curiosity?

3. Chuck writes: *Most of us are intrigued by the Holy Spirit. Like a moth to a lamp, His bright warmth attracts us. Our desire is to draw nearer, to know Him intimately. We long to enter into new and stimulating dimensions of His working—but yet we hold back* (page 6). Describe a question you have about the Holy Spirit that you've always wanted answered but you've never asked.

4. Look below at the questions that Chuck will address in this book. Which one interests or intrigues you the most? Why?
   * *Who is the Holy Spirit?*
   * *Why do I need the Spirit?*
   * *What does it mean to be filled with the Spirit?*
   * *How do I know I'm led by the Spirit?*
   * *How does the Spirit free me from sin?*
   * *Can I be prompted by the Spirit today?*
   * *Does the Spirit Heal today?*
   * *How can I know—really experience—the Spirit's power?*

One Thing to Do Today ∾

Pray. Simply ask the Lord to show you something about Himself through this careful look at His Spirit. Sample prayer: "Lord, You've promised that those who seek You will find You if we search for You with all our hearts. At the beginning of this study, I want to tell You today that I love You and want to know You in a deeper and more personal way. I don't want to just know facts about You, I want to know You. I don't want to miss one thing You have for our relationship. I'm excited for what I will discover about the Holy Spirit as I read this book.

"If there's anything in my heart that would be a barrier in growing deeper, please reveal it to me so that You have complete access to my life.

"I lay these cares at Your feet, Lord . . .

"Please help me in these areas today, Lord . . ."

∽ Chapter 1 ∽

WHO IS THE HOLY SPIRIT?

OVERVIEW

As one of His final acts on this earth before ascending into the clouds back to heaven, Jesus assured His followers that He was not going to leave them to face life alone. He would give us His own Spirit to live within us. Jesus called His Spirit, "the Helper." Get a fresh perspective in this chapter at all the ways the Helper ministers to you—even in ways you may not realize.

READ

Chapter 1 (pages 11–35); John 14:16–18

QUESTIONS

1. Did you ever connect the timing of Jesus' last days with the disciples with His promise that He would send His Spirit? Jesus wanted to continue the relationship with man, now through His Spirit. What do you think of that? How can your understanding of who Jesus is be transferred to your understanding of who His Spirit is? What characteristics do they share?

2. Why is it more beneficial for us to have the Holy Spirit than Christ Himself?

3. We can read in several places in the Bible that the Spirit indwelling us is God's guarantee to fulfill His promises today and His promises to come (1 Cor. 5:5; 2 Cor. 1:22). What encouragement or comfort does that give you?

ONE THING TO DO TODAY ∾

As you go about the details of your life today, consider the reality that you are not alone. Jesus promised not to leave you "orphaned" and so He gave you His Spirit to indwell you. If you know Him as Savior, you have God's Spirit with you. Talk to Him today as your Companion, Comforter, Savior, and Friend.

∞ Chapter 2 ∞
WHY DO I NEED THE SPIRIT?

OVERVIEW

In chapter 2, Chuck Swindoll gets personal. By first examining the radical difference the Spirit made in the lives of the disciples, the focus must naturally then turn to us. What difference has the Spirit made in your life? It's a question worth pondering.

READ

Chapter 2 (pages 37–57); John 16:13; Romans 12:1–2

QUESTIONS

1. The Spirit's main agenda is your transformation. In what ways have you changed (your mind, your character, your hope, your thinking, your perspective, etc.) since you came to Christ? Read Chuck's encouraging word: *Not only does that mean that the Spirit will make the Scriptures clear to you, but He will*

also take circumstances and give you insight into them. In other words, He transforms your mind. *He takes life's pressures and uses them to mature you.* He transforms your character. *He nurtures you. He comforts you when you're fractured with fear.* He transforms your hope. *He tells you there's another day coming when you can't see the end of the tunnel. He gives you a reason to go on when it looks like death is near.* He transforms your thinking. He transforms your heart. He transforms your perspective (pages 56–57).

2. On page 56, Chuck encourages us: *The third member of the Godhead, the invisible, albeit powerful, representation of deity,* is living inside your being. *You think you can't handle what life throws at you? You think you can't stand firm or when necessary stand alone in your life? You think you can't handle sin's temptations? Truth be told, you're right—you can't . . . alone. Neither could those disciples. But with the very power of God put into operation, you can handle it.* Testify to someone how God's Spirit has given you the ability and power to do something you couldn't have done on your own (victory over temptation, accomplishing something difficult, etc.). Even as you share this, do you feel God's Spirit stir faith in you?

One Thing to Do Today ∾

Where is your ability coming from in how you face the hard things in life today: trials, temptations, character decisions? Acknowledge to the Lord that you can't do this yourself. Perhaps you realize even now that you've been trying to do it on your own, and you turn now in surrender and ask the Lord's help. The Lord stands ready. Remember His Spirit is called "the Helper."

∾ **Chapter 3** ∾

What Does It Mean to Be Filled with the Spirit?

Overview

Most of life happens in the middle. Crises come but they don't usually last. Our tendency is to call out to the Lord in desperate times but the truth is, we need Him just as much in normal, everyday-life moments. The Spirit of God provides what we need at both times. Discover how to access the Spirit's power to live the Christian life—on hard days and all those in between.

READ

Chapter 3 (pages 59–88); Galatians 5:22–23; Ephesians 5:18–21

QUESTIONS

1. How do you know when you are filled? Perhaps a place to start is to look at the Galatians 5 list of the fruit of God's Spirit in control. Am I more loving? More patient? Did I persevere? Write the list in the back of your Bible, or in your journal, or someplace where you can frequently reference it. Ask the Lord to control your life in such a way that this fruit is expressed in a natural, daily way in your life.

2. Chuck tells us on pages 82–84 that we can tell we are filled by God's Spirit based on Ephesians 5:18–21: *When I'm filled with the Spirit, my heart is teachable. When I'm filled with the Spirit, my heart is melodious. When I'm filled with the Spirit, my heart is grateful. When I'm filled with the Spirit, my heart is humble.* Ask yourself, am I teachable? Joyful? Grateful? Humble? Ask the Lord to affirm your need of His Spirit to make these evidences tangible in your life.

3. In the following quote from pages 80–81, underline

the phrases that speak to areas of need in your life. Turn these needs into a prayer requesting the Spirit's help: *Over time, as we experience His filling, it becomes a constant part of our consciousness and our life. But we begin deliberately, slowly, and carefully. We need the Lord to enable us with discernment, to walk in obedience, to sense wrong when we encounter it and stay away from it. To keep us strong when temptation comes. To guard our tongues from saying the wrong things or saying too much or speaking too quickly. We need the Spirit to take our eyes, take our tongues, take our emotions, take our wills and use us, because we want to operate under His control on a continuing basis. This, my friend, is called the Christian walk.*

ONE THING TO DO TODAY ∞

Many a morning Chuck says he begins the day by sitting on the side of the bed, saying: *This is your day, Lord. I want to be at Your disposal. I have no idea what these next twenty-four hours will contain. But before I sip my first cup of coffee, and even before I get dressed, I want You to know that from this moment on throughout this day, I'm Yours, Lord. Help me to lean on You, to draw strength from You, and to have You fill my mind and my thoughts. Take control of my senses so that I am literally filled with Your presence and empowered with Your energy. I want to be Your tool,*

Your vessel today. I can't make it happen. And so I'm saying,
Lord, fill me with Your Spirit today.

You can begin your day today with a similar prayer.
"Lord, enable me today to live out the authentic Christian
life for Your glory." Customize it with your own details
depending on the needs of your particular day.

༄ Chapter 4 ༄
How Do I Know I'm Led by the Spirit?

OVERVIEW

None of us wants to miss God's best for our lives. We
all want to be held on a steady course by His guiding
presence. So, where do we find that direction, that
leading? This is the work of the Holy Spirit, the Helper
who comes alongside us. Allow the Lord to lead you into
His truth as you read more on this personal matter of
how He directs our lives.

READ

Chapter 4 (pages 89–119); Ephesians 6:6; Hebrews 11:6

QUESTIONS

1. Think back over your life, both before and since you came to Christ as Savior. Can you look back over your life experiences and recall a time when you see now that the Lord was leading you?

2. Consider how the Spirit has been at work in your life in recent days. Chuck lists examples of the Spirit's work in the bulleted list on page 92—can you identify with any of these experiences?

3. On page 90 we read: *If we could see the Spirit at work in our lives, we would realize that in every situation God is doing hundreds of things we cannot see and do not know.* How does this encourage your faith? Consider encouraging a friend with this quote and then telling that person how you see God at work in his or her life.

ONE THING TO DO TODAY ∞

For what are you waiting on God right now? A decision you need to make? A situation that needs resolution? A relationship that needs restoration? Believe that God is leading you to a conclusion in this matter. Look for His hand in opportunities and be willing to do what He shows you to do.

∞ Chapter 5 ∞

HOW DOES THE SPIRIT FREE ME FROM SIN?

OVERVIEW

Sin in all its ugliness has a grip on us that we cannot escape, enslaving us in patterns of thoughts and behaviors that grieve the Lord and hurt us. Without the Spirit's indwelling and constant help, sin would wrap its customized, personalized chains around us. It would destroy us . . . in a flash. As it is, sin's devastating effect on our personal lives is beyond what any of us would imagine. It's time to surrender our dark side to the Spirit's control.

READ

Chapter 5 (pages 121–143); Romans 6:6, 12–13

QUESTIONS

1. Have you ever felt trapped by your own sin? Have you tried to stop doing a certain sin, only to be defeated by your own dark side? Do you feel like you're a victim to your sin? Rather than pushing these thoughts aside, face them head on. Sinners need a Savior. Be grateful you have one!

2.   Agree or disagree? *Truth be told . . . you don't have to sin. You know why you sin? Because you want to!*

3.   Consider a sin that you often struggle with. Now read what Chuck says on pages 136–137: *Romans 6:14 declares, "Sin shall not be master over you, for you are not under law but under grace." . . . I like the way the J. B. Phillips paraphrase renders the same verse: "Like men [and women] rescued from certain death, put yourselves in God's hands as weapons of good for his own purposes. For sin is not meant to be your master." . . . Are you hearing this? Then stop the habit of obeying your former drill instructor! He's no longer in charge of you.*

One Thing to Do Today ⌇

Identify that one thing that keeps you down. Surrender it to the Spirit's control. That sin isn't your master anymore—God is!

⌇ Chapter 6 ⌇

CAN I BE PROMPTED BY THE SPIRIT TODAY?

OVERVIEW

The only way God can communicate with us at times is through unidentified inner promptings (UIPs)—seen at times as conviction or assurance or direction or reassurance or encouragement. Let's stop calling these things "coincidences" and "hunches" and "feelings." Identify them as the work of the Spirit. God is communicating with you through His Spirit.

READ

Chapter 6 (pages 145–163); Proverbs 4:23

QUESTIONS

1. On pages 151–157, Chuck described the unidentified inner promptings (UIPs) that Elijah and Paul experienced. Name another person in the Bible who experienced a "UIP" from the Lord. Describe a time when you felt you experienced a UIP.

2. Do you wonder at times if it's the Lord leading or if it's a good turn of events? Chuck's bulleted list about when to resist inner promptings (page 159) is wise to consider. Do any of these cautions strike a chord in you today? He continues: *Those are all promptings that you shouldn't pursue. However, the flip side of that is when you are confident it is from the Lord . . . go for it!*

3. God often says, "I am with you." You know in advance that if you take the journey that's in front of you, there will be trials. But the "gentle rustling" of the Lord says, "I am with you. I will give you the strength." Such UIPs can be wonderfully reassuring. Recall a time in your life when the Lord affirmed His presence with you through His Spirit. How does this memory give you faith and confidence for today's struggle?

ONE THING TO DO TODAY ⁓

Heed Chuck's advice (from page 153) today: *If there's anything that troubles me about our culture and our times, it is the noise and the pace of it all. Those things work against the voice of God quietly speaking to reach us. I warn you about being so busy you miss His voice. Back off. Take time to listen. God's voice may be in the earthquake or the fire. There are messages there. But often, His inner promptings will come in the deep well of our spirit, for He simply says, "Yes, go there" or "Wait," or "No. Stay away from that." Slow down. Cool your jets. Take time to listen.*

∞ Chapter 7 ∞
DOES THE SPIRIT HEAL TODAY?

OVERVIEW

God is doing some of His best work in us in the time it takes to heal. Almost imperceptibly, we become people with keener sensitivity, a broader base of understanding, and a longer fuse! Patience is a byproduct of lingering pain. So is tolerance with others and obedience before God. It is difficult to know how to classify these characteristics, but for lack of a better title, let's call the whole package *Spirit-given wisdom*. Does God heal? Yes, He does. He also purposefully uses pain.

READ

Chapter 7 (pages 165–192); James 5:3-5; Psalm 119:67, 71; Ecclesiastes 3:1-3

QUESTIONS

1. Have you ever prayed for someone's healing and they got well? Ever prayed and they did not get well— and perhaps died? How do you mentally, spiritually, and emotionally process these events?

2. Do you know someone (or perhaps are you someone) who has suffered with long-term pain? What is your response to Chuck's statement: *Affliction has now entered your life, and even though you would much prefer to have it over with, it has not ended. The pain you are forced to endure is reshaping and remaking you deep within* (page 186)?

3. Chuck writes: *There is no such thing as "luck" or "coincidence" or "fate" to the child of God. Behind our every experience is our loving, sovereign Lord. He is continually working things out according to His infinite plan and purpose. And that includes our suffering* (page 191). What do you think of this statement? Is it freeing, troubling, comforting, other_____?

ONE THING TO DO TODAY ∽

In this chapter, Chuck describes "Five Suffering Laws" regarding sin, sickness, health, and healing:

Law #1: There are two classifications of sin.
Law #2: Original sin introduced suffering, illness, and death to the human race.
Law #3: Sometimes there is a direct relationship between personal sins and sickness.

Law #4: Sometimes there is no *relationship between personal sins and sickness.*

Law #5: It is not God's will that everyone be healed.

And its corollary: Sometimes it is God's will that someone is healed.

Read each one again. Write the laws in the back of your Bible. Sure as the world, you are going to run into someone who will wonder why he or she (or a loved one) is not being healed. Maybe God will use your words to calm that person's anxiety and remove his or her confusion.

∾ Chapter 8 ∾

HOW CAN I EXPERIENCE THE POWER OF THE SPIRIT?

OVERVIEW

The most powerful force in your life as a Christian is something you can't even see. It is so powerful it holds you eternally till Christ comes and secures your destiny, ushering you right into eternity. In the meantime, He is ready to work within you, transforming your life. The Spirit's power is waiting to be used. The Spirit's power in control of the life of a believer is nothing short of phenomenal.

Study Guide

READ
Chapter 8 (pages 193–214); John 1:12; Romans 8:16–17

QUESTIONS

1. How would you complete these two sentences?
   I am a Christian because _____.
   I am filled with the Spirit when _____.
   As a follower of Christ, what now are your expectations regarding the Spirit's work in your life as it relates to: how He leads you? how He gives you the power to live a godly life? how He heals you?

2. Look at the bulleted list on pages 199–200. Which characteristics in the list stir your faith? Encourage you? Comfort you? If the Spirit is ministering to you through this list, copy it down in the back of your Bible to return to in the future. These are facts—evidences of God's work in you at your salvation.

3. Now look at the bulleted list on pages 202–203. This is a list of the evidence of God's Spirit at work in you because you are cooperating with Him. This list is optional in the Christian life—as in, your choice. Copy this list and put it in a place where you see it often and where it will help you choose to be Spirit-filled on a daily basis. Which points do you need to remind yourself of today?

ONE THING TO DO TODAY ∽

As you finish this study, Chuck makes one request: *Can I ask you to do one thing? Simply sit in silence for a few moments before the Lord. Looking back, you may see things that need attention. Or it may make you smile as you realize how gracious God has been. When you think ahead, you may feel twinges of fear. It's a great moment to tell Him that. Ask Him for reassurance and a sense of peace. Ask Him to fill your life with His Spirit, surrendering all that you say and do, all that you are, to His control* (page 214).

Charles R. Swindoll has devoted over four decades to two passions: an unwavering commitment to the practical communication and application of God's Word, and an untiring devotion to seeing lives transformed by God's grace. Chuck graduated *magna cum laude* from Dallas Theological Seminary and has since been honored with four doctorates. For his teaching on *Insight for Living*, he has received the Program of the Year award and the Hall of Fame award from the National Religious Broadcasters as well as multiple book awards. He and his wife of over half a century, Cynthia, live in Texas.

Share Your Thoughts

With the Author: Your comments will be forwarded to the author when you send them to *zauthor@zondervan.com*.

With Zondervan: Submit your review of this book by writing to *zreview@zondervan.com*.

Free Online Resources at
www.zondervan.com

Zondervan AuthorTracker: Be notified whenever your favorite authors publish new books, go on tour, or post an update about what's happening in their lives at www.zondervan.com/authortracker.

Daily Bible Verses and Devotions: Enrich your life with daily Bible verses or devotions that help you start every morning focused on God. Visit www.zondervan.com/newsletters.

Free Email Publications: Sign up for newsletters on Christian living, academic resources, church ministry, fiction, children's resources, and more. Visit www.zondervan.com/newsletters.

Zondervan Bible Search: Find and compare Bible passages in a variety of translations at www.zondervanbiblesearch.com.

Other Benefits: Register yourself to receive online benefits like coupons and special offers, or to participate in research.

ZONDERVAN®

ZONDERVAN.com/
AUTHORTRACKER
follow your favorite authors